PRAISE FOR *THE MAP*

"Part thriller story, part step-by-step call to action, *The Map* will be absolutely life changing for men. This insightful work will inspire and equip every man to follow the journey of Jesus and become not only a man of submission but a man of godly strength and courage."

— JEFF AND SHAUNTI FELDHAHN
Best-selling authors of *For Men Only* and *For Women Only*

"The spiritual punch of C. S. Lewis, written in the style of a Jason Bourne thriller. I can't imagine a more powerful, readable combination."

— ROBERT LEWIS
Founder, Men's Fraternity

"In a tale filled with danger, mystery, and intrigue, David Murrow reveals a hidden map embedded in Scripture that men have followed or ignored to their success or their demise."

— ERIC SWANSON
Leadership Network

"What kind of fool would embark on a journey without a map? Yet men tackle the most important journey of their lives—the journey to manhood—without one. No wonder so many men are adrift. This book provides the map that men so desperately need."

— DAVE BILLINGTON
Composer, "You are Awesome in this Place"

"Murrow has lit yet another rare candle that illuminates a mysterious, neglected, and sometimes vilified portion of a man's unique soul."

— PAUL COUGHLIN
Author, *No More Christian Nice Guy*

"Absolutely brilliant! David Murrow has written a masterpiece that could revolutionize men's ministry and the way we disciple men. I love this book—I'm just jealous I didn't write it myself."

> — RICK JOHNSON
> Best-selling author of *The Power of a Man* and *Better Dads, Stronger Sons*

"Murrow has created a whole new literary genre—the spiritual formation thriller. *The Map* mixes international intrigue with the Gospel of Matthew to create a book on masculine spirituality that guys I know will actually read. I can't wait to get this into their hands!"

> — DR. ROBB REDMAN
> Dean and Vice President
> Associate Professor of Theology and Ministry
> Multnomah Biblical Seminary
> Portland, OR

"As a college pastor, I think young men will love this book. I look forward to using it to challenge many young men."

> — STEVE LUTZ
> College Pastor, Penn State University
> Director, Commontary.com

"Who else could give us a book that reads like a novella, hooks you like a largemouth bass, and then delivers a fresh vision of manhood that challenges you at the deepest levels? I'm going to give *The Map* the strongest possible recommendation to the men of Saddleback."

> — KENNY LUCK
> Founder, Every Man Ministries
> Men's Pastor, Saddleback Church
> Author of *Risk, Dream, Fight* and the Every Man Bible Studies

"A book written in the style of John Grisham, but with substance that will guide your life as a man. I can't wait for the men of my church to read it."

— STEVE SONDERMAN
Associate Pastor, Elmbrook
Church Men's Ministry
Founder, Top Gun Ministry

"Men's books? I've read them all. But never one like *The Map*. It's amazing in its approach, uniqueness, simplicity, and insight."

— BILL PERKINS
Author, *Six Battles Every Man
Must Win*

"David Murrow found something that millions of others missed: a map to manhood, hidden in the New Testament. This book is going to change the way the church develops its men."

— MARK GUNGOR
Author, *Laugh Your Way to a Better
Marriage*

"We tell men to follow Jesus, but what does that really mean? David Murrow helps men find the balance between Christ's tough and tender sides. *The Map* shows us when to be like "table-tipping Jesus" and when to be submissive."

— BRAD STINE
Comedian, Actor, Author

The Map

The Map

THE WAY OF ALL GREAT MEN

DAVID MURROW

THOMAS NELSON
Since 1798

NASHVILLE DALLAS MEXICO CITY RIO DE JANEIRO

Published in Nashville, Tennessee, by Thomas Nelson. Thomas Nelson is a registered trademark of Thomas Nelson, Inc.

Published in association with WordServe Literary, 10152 Knoll Circle, Highlands Ranch, CO 80130, www.wordserveliterary.com.

Thomas Nelson, Inc., titles may be purchased in bulk for educational, business, fund-raising, or sales promotional use. For information, please e-mail SpecialMarkets@ThomasNelson.com.

Unless otherwise marked, Scripture quotations are taken from THE HOLY BIBLE: NEW INTERNATIONAL VERSION®. © 1973, 1978, 1984 by International Bible Society. Used by permission of Zondervan. All rights reserved.

Scripture quotations marked CEV are taken from THE CONTEMPORARY ENGLISH VERSION. © 1991 by the American Bible Society. Used by permission.

Scripture quotations marked ESV are taken from THE ENGLISH STANDARD VERSION. © 2001 by Crossway Bibles, a division of Good News Publishers.

Scripture quotations marked KJV are taken from The King James Version. Public Domain.

Scripture quotations marked MSG are taken from *The Message* by Eugene H. Peterson. © 1993, 1994, 1995, 1996, 2000. Used by permission of NavPress Publishing Group. All rights reserved.

Scripture quotations marked NKJV are taken from THE NEW KING JAMES VERSION. © 1982 by Thomas Nelson, Inc. Used by permission. All rights reserved.

Library of Congress Cataloging-in-Publication Data

Murrow, David.
    The Map : the way of all great men / David Murrow.
       p. cm.
    Includes bibliographical references.
    ISBN 978-0-7852-2762-5 (pbk.)
    1. Christian men—Religious life. 2. Men (Christian theology) I. Title.
BV4528.2.M87 2009
248.8'42—dc22   2009042344

Printed in the United States of America

10 11 12 13 14 RRD 5 4

CONTENTS

INTRODUCTION

In 2005 I wrote a book titled *Why Men Hate Going to Church*.[1] It was based on a simple premise: the modern church has become too feminine. As a result, men are going passive—or going away.

To everyone's surprise (including mine), the book became an inspirational bestseller. Many men loved it, but some men were deeply disturbed by it. A lot of the things I had labeled in the book as "feminine" were profoundly meaningful to these guys. They said things such as,

- "I cried like a baby when I met Jesus. I didn't care about my manhood."
- "I love sharing in my small group of guys. I find healing there."
- "There's nothing wrong with getting a hug from the brothers in my small group."
- "I left my tough-guy exterior at the foot of the cross."
- "We're most like Christ not when we're tough, but when we're tender."
- "It's good to get emotional during praise and worship."
- "I'm proud to say that I love Jesus."

One time a guy came storming up to the book table after I had spoken to a men's group. "David, you keep talking about gentleness and meekness being feminine," he said, voice trembling with emotion. "But the Bible commands us to be gentle and meek. The manliest guy in the room isn't the toughest; he's the one who's most loving."

He was right—but so was I. Church *is* too feminine. But if a man is to become whole (emotionally and spiritually), he must shed his macho pretensions and do things that many men would consider *girly*.

I've come to realize that my first book was correct—but incomplete. The softer virtues *do* play a vital role in a man's spiritual development. Christian men can't simply ignore commands such as "Turn the other cheek" because they seem unmanly. Every guy needs a good boo-hoo now and then.

But if a man gets too acquainted with his softer side, he risks becoming a softy. This is a huge problem in the church today. Authors such as John Eldredge, Bill Perkins, Mark Gungor, and Paul Coughlin have all noted the emasculating effect that modern Christianity is having on men.

So where is the balance point? How can men get in touch with their feminine sides without becoming *feminized*?

One day I stumbled across the answer. I discovered the ancient map to manhood—in a most unexpected way.

PART ONE

The Discovery

Chapter 1

OUT OF THE BLACK

My eyes snapped open, but I saw nothing. I blinked—and paid the price. My eyelids felt as though they were lined with sandpaper. I tried to sit up, but pain shot through my legs. Slowly I rolled onto my back, trying to remember where I was. Through a slit in the roof, I saw a black sky dotted with stars. I knew just two things: I was awake, and I was alive.

I pressed the glow button on my watch: 4:32 a.m. What had wakened me? *The rooster.* His crowing was like a poorly timed snooze alarm, with just enough of an interval between cock-a-doodle-doos to lull me back to sleep and then jerk me back to consciousness.

Why is there a rooster? I heard something stirring— maybe three meters from my head. I lay very still, trying not to breathe. Something metal scraped against a stone floor. Then I heard the sound of a body shifting its weight, followed by a heavy exhale. I felt as though I was in danger, but I had no idea why.

My thoughts began to clear. I was in a barn. Somewhere in Greece. This was not an American-style barn with a steep, pitched roof and a spacious hayloft. My shelter was a crude, single-story, stone-walled structure that had been built around the time young George Washington was chopping down cherry trees.

I soon realized that the sounds that had frightened me came not from an assassin but from a draft horse, dragging an iron shoe across worn pavement. Moments later my nose was assaulted by the smell of freshly dropped manure. *Yes, I'm definitely in a barn*, I thought.

I'm not in the habit of sleeping with livestock, but stranded travelers take whatever accommodations they can get. It was coming back to me: I had no transportation, no cell phone, and I couldn't speak a word of Greek. I was hiding from men who were trying to either help me or kill me—I wasn't sure.

I shared my crude accommodations with the horse, a cow, a donkey, and my travel companion—an Anglican priest from Wales who went by the name Benson. The vicar had been snoring proficiently through the night, but at the moment he was silent. If the cock had awakened him, he showed no sign of it. The two of us shared our bed of straw with a number of scurrying creatures, probably mice or rats. Their constant motion had kept me on edge all night.

The barn was located in the tiny Greek monastic state of Mount Athos. The priest and I had journeyed to this backwater in search of a treasure map.

Now, stop laughing. This was no *Pirates of the Caribbean* treasure map. This particular map led to something even more valuable than gold. I wasn't even sure the map existed. But if the rumor was true, we were on the verge of a discovery so explosive it had the potential to shake the foundations of Christianity—or lead to its rebirth.

I rose stiffly and stumbled out of the barn with two goals: (1) tap a kidney and (2) kill the rooster. As I stood in the barnyard working on my first goal, my eyes scanned the dark countryside. I took a moment to assess my current situation: eight thousand miles from home, searching for a map that may or may not exist—seeking information from a Greek Orthodox monk who may or may not know anything—hiding from men who may or may not be trying to kill me. My life was a bubbling cauldron of uncertainty.

I'm no Indiana Jones. I'm a father of three, whose idea of adventure is booking a hotel on Priceline.com. I was drawn into this expedition because the map supposedly had something to do with Jesus Christ and the path to manhood—topics that I've studied extensively and written on. My goal was to find the map and share it with the world. And what the heck—if the discovery led to me writing an international bestseller, I was sure the Lord wouldn't mind.

By now the rooster had gone silent, so I decided to spare him. Back inside, the barn seemed darker, and the smells were even more pungent. To my left, the priest was snoring again, but it was so dark I couldn't make out his form. One of the animals was stirring in its stall—or was it something else? I held very still, fighting the eerie feeling that someone was watching me. Then a thought occurred: *Do roosters suddenly go silent once their morning recital begins?*

Meanwhile, Father Nigel Benson began snuffling again. I felt safer with him nearby, even though he was about as threatening as the Pillsbury Dough Boy.

My mind wandered back to the first time I met Benson. We were in Wales. It was about five months ago, on February 1.

I stepped out of the warm church building into a raw Welsh night. An unkind wind blew off the Atlantic. Rain spattered onto the parking lot under an ebony sky that had surrendered its last ray of light hours ago.

Though the night was chilly, my heart was warmed by the love I had felt that evening, addressing a crowd of about 120 at St. Mary's Parish in Cardiff, Wales. They'd come to hear a lecture titled "Why Men Hate Going to Church," based on a book I'd written a few years before. The lack of men in U.S. churches is a bother, but in the U.K. it's a crippling epidemic. I'd found an enthusiastic group eager for my message. I was just walking out to my rental car when I heard a voice from behind.

"Mr. Murrow?" the voice said.

I turned quickly. "Yes, who's there?"

"I was inside, listening to your address. Very interesting."

"You startled me," I said.

"I apologize. I just had to speak to you. Alone."

A chill ran up my back. It had nothing to do with the breeze. "What is this about?" I asked defensively.

"Can you meet me tomorrow? I have some very important information that I must share with you."

"Who are you?" I asked.

"Apologies. My name is Benson—Nigel Benson—and I am a priest living at the vicarage at Churchstoke, about seventy miles north of here. Like many ministers, I am fascinated by your topic. Over the years, I've had only a wee bit of luck engaging men in the church. I came down to Cardiff to hear you speak."

His voice had the soothing tone of a minister, and my unease began melting into a tentative trust. Benson was a bowling ball of a man, about sixty years old, short, with broad shoulders. Close-cropped gray hair framed a large head. A pair of badly dated eyeglasses perched on his bulbous nose.

Large, solid hands sprang from the arms of his mackintosh. He held an Englishman's black umbrella over his head.

"Thank you for coming," I said. "What's this information you spoke of?"

Benson looked down at the wet pavement. "Mr. Murrow, I can't tell you that because I don't know what it is. I was sent by a man named Spiro."

"Why didn't Mr. Spiro come tonight?"

"It's *Father* Spiro," Benson said. "He is in his nineties and in failing health. I would have brought him along, but he's recovering from pneumonia. He doesn't use a computer and can hardly hear to use the phone. But he has read your book and he's keen to meet you."

We were silent for a moment. I didn't know what to say, so I finally joked, "Well, it's good to know I have a ninety-year-old admirer."

"Oh, he's no admirer," Benson said. "He thinks your conclusions are rubbish."

Rubbish? I felt as though I'd been sucker-punched. After a few seconds, I recovered enough to ask, "If he thinks my book is trash, then why does he want to meet me?"

"Because you're the first writer in a generation to address the subject of the missing men in the church," Benson said. "You have a platform. Spiro wants to show you the *real* reason men are leaving the church, so you can share it with your readers."

The real reason? My mind was red with indignation. *Who does this Spiro think he is? Has he done the research? How dare he call my work rubbish!*

Before I could answer, Benson continued. "Mr. Murrow, I checked your itinerary online. You are scheduled to speak tomorrow night in Shrewsbury. That's just twenty miles from

7

the vicarage in Churchstoke. We could easily meet Father Spiro in the morning and have you to Shrewsbury in plenty of time for tea. Now, where are you staying?"

"At the Nag's Head." The words tumbled out before I could stop them.

"Very well. I'll meet you in the lobby at eight o'clock sharp. Good evening, Mr. Murrow." The vicar turned and melted into the night.

The morning dawned under dripping gray skies. I sat in the hotel restaurant, waiting for my English breakfast to be served. A cold rain fogged the windowpanes that faced the street. In the corner a welcoming fire chased away the last remnants of evening chill.

I had spent the morning trying to decide if I should meet Benson or simply jump in the car and head to Shrewsbury. My left brain cried, *He's a nut. It's going to be a colossal waste of time. Stick with the schedule.*

Unfortunately, the restaurant was short-staffed, and my breakfast was delayed. A harried waitress finally set my plate down at ten till eight. I shoveled in a few bites of egg, tomato, and sausage and then decided to make my escape before the priest arrived. I paid the check and was headed for the door when a stout man in a black mackintosh walked into the dining room, shaking the water off a large umbrella.

"Good morning, Mr. Murrow," the man said. "Ready to go?" Benson's manner was so insistent that I nodded involuntarily. "Where is your suitcase?" he asked.

"Oh, it's at the front desk," I said. In my attempt to flee, I'd almost forgotten that I'd placed my belongings with the staff during breakfast. "I'll go get it," I said.

"Do you have an umbrella?" Benson asked. I showed him my empty hands.

"Very well. Let me have your key and I'll open the boot for you. No sense in you spending one extra second out in this monsoon," he said.

Against my better judgment, I handed the key to my rental car to a character I barely knew. As I retrieved my luggage, I wondered if I'd ever see the four-cylinder Vauxhall again.

I walked out of the hotel into a punishing rain. Fortunately, I had parked near the door. The trunk (or boot, as it's called in the U.K.) was already open and I tossed in my suitcase, slamming it closed as fast as I could. Since I'm an American, without thinking I ran to the left side of the car and jumped in, expecting to be in the driver's seat. Instead, Benson sat at the wheel, which of course was on the right. The priest turned the key, and the engine roared to life. "No sense in you driving, Mr. Murrow. The weather's dodgy, and you don't know the way. Save your strength for your talk tonight."

Before I could object, Benson had the sedan in gear, and we were barreling down the narrow streets of Cardiff. *Well, at least he didn't steal the car*, I thought. In the background, BBC radio was carrying a story about a massive accident on the rain-slicked M4 highway.

"So your name is Nigel?" I asked.

"Yes, that's what my mum called me, but ever since primary school I've gone by Benson. There were five Nigels in my year one class, so the headmaster put an end to the madness by referring to us by our last names."

"It's tough being a David too," I said. "One time I was in a history class with four Davids. Our teacher had a glass eye. When he called on 'David,' you could never tell which one of us he was looking at."

Benson snickered. Then the car fell silent, except for the clapping of the wipers and a radio report on a financial scandal in the House of Lords. As we drove, the rain let up somewhat.

I finally broke the silence. "Benson, tell me more about this priest we're going to meet."

"Father Spiro? Well, I think I mentioned that he's quite old and fragile. He's originally from Greece. He fled to England during World War II, just before Greece fell to Hitler. He carried some Jewish blood and feared for his safety. He's well versed in ancient Semitic languages.

"Father Spiro eventually ended up in Wales, where he served as a parish priest for twenty-five years. He continued to be a popular vicar into his eighties. He still lives in the vicarage at Churchstoke and had been quite independent until about a month ago when he got pneumonia."

"How old did you say he is?" I asked.

"Ninety-four. Still sharp minded. A good wit. His sermons were always popular because they were so funny," Benson said.

"And you said that he read my book but didn't think much of it."

"He deeply appreciates what you're trying to do, but he thinks your conclusions are off." Benson tapped the steering wheel nervously and then added, "Father Spiro was never one to hold back an opinion."

I kept a respectful demeanor, but inside I was thinking, *What a colossal waste of time this is going to be. A ninety-four-year-old vicar is going to tell me why he thinks men are skipping church. He's probably going to tell me it's too much trouble to hook up the horse and buggy on Sunday morning.*

I stared out the passenger side window. Thick hedgerows

bisected lush pastures. Rain had been falling for weeks, turning the land impossibly green. After a few minutes of silence, Benson spoke. "Well, this is Churchstoke. We'll be at the vicarage in a few minutes." I was amazed—the U.K. is so small compared to Alaska. I felt as though we had only been driving a few minutes, and already we were nearing our destination.

The vicarage was a converted English public house two blocks from St. Stephen's, the village church. The building housed the church offices and several apartments for priests, both active and retired. The structure looked to be from the mid-1800s, with thick, brown walls and a clay tile roof. Spindly vines grew up the south wall. The windows had been upgraded to energy-efficient double-pane sliders.

The rain had stopped. Benson and I got out and walked across sodden cobbles into the building. The priest led me up the stairs to the parish offices, where a prim secretary sat guard.

"Good morning, Rosalind," Benson said with characteristic English reserve.

Rosalind looked over her glasses without smiling. "Oh, Benson, have you heard the terrible news?"

"No, what is it?" Benson asked.

"Father Spiro is dead."

Chapter 2

DISARRAY

Benson sat motionless, staring down at a steaming cup of tea. His large hands were folded in his lap. I sat across the table, not knowing what to say.

We were seated at the Long Acre, a pub three blocks from the vicarage. It had been less than sixteen hours since I first laid eyes on this man, but I felt his loss deeply. Maybe God had set me on this wild goose chase to comfort a man who had consoled so many hurting people in the past.

I finally spoke. "You and Father Spiro must have been very close."

"Yes, but there's no time to mourn. I'm trying to figure if Spiro was murdered."

Murdered? You've got to be kidding. Benson was not grieving; he was playing amateur detective! I hid my skepticism enough to ask, "What makes you suspect foul play? He was ninety-four years old, right? He had pneumonia."

Benson was quick to answer: "Spiro was a fastidious man. I visited his apartment yesterday morning, and it was as tidy as the grounds of Windsor Castle. Yet today a number of his books are in disarray. That would indicate that someone went through them."

"Well, what if he was studying at the time of his death?"

"Spiro was bedridden with pneumonia. Rosalind says he spent the day sleeping. It looks to me as though someone pulled his books down, looked at them, and put them back in the wrong order."

I was unconvinced, but I decided to play along. "Will there be a police investigation? Or an autopsy?"

"I doubt it. As you said, he *was* ninety-four years old."

The lunch crowd was starting to file out of the Long Acre. I was also feeling the need to move along, but I decided to humor the priest a bit longer. "Let's assume for a minute that Spiro's death was not natural. Who on earth would want to kill him?"

"Mr. Murrow, I haven't told you everything Spiro told me. I didn't want to speak for him. But now it's apparent that I'll have to do just that." Benson fixed his gaze on me and lowered his voice. "Spiro appeared to be a humble priest, but he actually had a number of high-level government and religious contacts around the world. It's rumored that he played a role in the formation of the Israeli government after 1948. He used to take long holidays to Greece and the Middle East in the summer, doing unspecified research."

Benson blew over his steaming teacup and took a quick sip. "Spiro had observed the decline of Christianity in Europe over his lifetime, and he thought it was due to the withdrawal of a certain kind of man from religious life. When Spiro was a boy, working men with calloused hands would become priests. But during the twentieth century, seminaries began to attract what he called "eggheads, whelps, and softies." Once the priests went velvety, the men in the pews lost respect for them. Fathers stopped bringing their families to church, and that broke the multigenerational chain of faith.

"When Spiro found your book, he agreed with many of your observations, but he felt that your ultimate conclusion fell short of the mark. He was keen to share his findings with you."

"What findings?" I asked.

"Father Spiro told me that he and his colleagues had uncovered something of inestimable worth—a long-lost document that was key to transforming millions of men. He referred to it as a map, or a diagram." Benson looked down and then leaned forward and whispered, "Spiro implied that this document may have been written by one of the twelve apostles."

In a flash my curiosity yielded to skepticism. *Murder? Secret documents? The twelve apostles?* I've seen this movie; it's called *The Da Vinci Code*, and I didn't really care for it. I was not about to surrender myself to this lunatic theory. My impatience boiled to the surface. "Benson, this is crazy. I have a very hard time believing someone would want to murder a ninety-four-year-old priest in failing health."

"Mr. Murrow, do you believe in the spiritual world? Angels, demons, and the like?"

"Yes," I said cautiously.

"So do I. I was skeptical for years, but a trip to Africa changed my mind."

Benson repositioned his teacup, gathering his thoughts. "Let's say you're commander of the army of darkness— Lucifer himself. Your goal is to stop the kingdom of light from advancing. Is this an acceptable analogy for you?"

"Go on," I said.

"One day someone stumbles upon the ancient training manual for soldiers of the light. It's been lost for centuries. This little document is the key to awakening, preparing, and deploying the sleeping giant in the church—laymen." Benson placed his palms on the table. "You're the devil. What would your strategy be?"

"I'd do everything within my power to keep that document hidden," I said.

Benson's eyes locked onto mine. "Jesus described the evil one as a murderer and a thief. Why is it so hard to imagine that one of his henchmen killed Father Spiro and stole the training manual?"

I was still skeptical. "Have you ever seen this manual—this map?" I asked.

"No, but Spiro was convinced of its existence. Whoever went through his belongings must have been seeking the map, or a clue as to its whereabouts." Benson went silent and then muttered under his breath, "There's no telling how far they went to extract the information from Father Spiro."

I could feel myself succumbing to Benson's persuasive powers, but my rational mind muscled to the fore. "Benson, I came to the U.K. to give a few lectures and sign some books. Secret maps and murder mysteries are not on my itinerary."

"Mr. Murrow, you may think I'm daft. But I'm asking you to take a chance. Help me find that map. It could lead to the very outcome you seek: the spiritual awakening of millions of men."

The priest reached into his vest pocket. "I have the name of a man in Jerusalem. Because Spiro did not use a computer, he asked me to send multiple e-mails to this man. Spiro's messages concerned some recovered Hebrew documents. I'm convinced that these documents are the key to finding the map." Benson pushed a folded piece of paper across the table. "Please contact him at your earliest opportunity. I'll keep investigating the situation here."

"Why don't you contact him?" I asked.

"He told me not to," Benson said, tapping on the paper for emphasis. "About a year ago, he sent me a letter by post, requesting that no one from the vicarage contact him again. Something about our religious differences. However, I think he might answer you, because you're a layman."

Benson stood and extended his hand. "Thank you so much for coming. Shrewsbury is just twenty miles east of here. Go north to the first roundabout; then follow the arrows."

I rose to my feet, shook Benson's hand, and held the paper in front of his face. "No promises," I said.

I smiled, grabbed my jacket, and walked out of the pub into brilliant sunshine.

Chapter 3

THE LETTER

So much for global warming. The calendar said April 22, but huge, wet snowflakes were falling on my yard, my deck, and my roof. In Alaska, winter is a jealous lover, reluctant to loosen her grip.

I had planned to go bicycling today, but that was now out of the question. So I spent the afternoon in my office, attacking a flurry of paperwork that had snowballed over the course of winter.

I was buried in one of my least favorite tasks—organizing and filing my receipts—when I came across a neatly folded piece of paper. I recognized it immediately as the note that Benson had given me at the pub almost three months ago. I'd stuffed it into my wallet without even looking at it. Before pitching it into the trash, I took a peek. The note read:

Please contact Mr. Isaac Kassif at this address: Kassif48@ yevnet.co.il.

I stared at the note, thinking, *I can throw this in the trash, or I can write Mr. Kassif an e-mail, which will allow me to put off filing those blasted receipts for five more minutes.* So I opened my laptop and composed the following message:

Dear Mr. Kassif:

I received your e-mail address from Rev. Nigel Benson, an associate of Rev. Spiro of Churchstoke, Wales, in the United Kingdom. He asked me to contact you regarding some research you and Spiro were doing. I'm the author of the books *Why Men Hate Going to Church* and *How Women Help Men Find God.* I also represent Church for Men, an organization that helps Christian congregations reconnect with their men and boys.

If you'd like to contact me, please respond to this e-mail or visit my Web site, www.churchformen.com.

Warmest regards,

David Murrow

Weeks passed with no reply from Kassif. The snow was gone and the robins were in full song the day a letter arrived postmarked "Jerusalem." The envelope bore no return address, but I knew instantly who had sent it.

Dear Mr. Murrow:

Greetings from Jerusalem. Peace to you and your family. Please forgive me for not responding by e-mail as you requested. I think a paper letter is best. Also, I ask you please do not send me any more e-mail messages.

I want to meet you in New York on July 12. I will be in America attending a conference. You will stay at Crowne

Plaza Hotel on Broadway. An associate will pick you up at
the airport.

Shalom,

Isaac Kassif

Inside the envelope was a round-trip plane ticket from
Anchorage to New York, in my name, departing July 11 and
returning July 13.

Wow. I felt as though I'd stepped into a Tom Clancy
novel. *This is the weirdest thing that's ever happened to me*, I
thought. I went to my calendar, expecting it to be full—but
the week of July 11 was pure white space.

I took a couple of days to seek advice. I prayed. My wife
(who's braver than I am) was amazingly supportive. I'm not
sure how one is supposed to make a decision like this, but in
the end my gut just told me to go. Nineteen days later, I was
on my way to New York City.

Newark Liberty Airport was buzzing with activity the afternoon of July 12. I'd flown the red-eye out of Anchorage, with
a change of planes in Seattle. I was so groggy I almost missed
the driver holding up my name on a small whiteboard. *David
Marrow.* Oh well. I hoped his driving was better than his
spelling.

Wow. A limo from the airport? This I could get used to. My
driver, Salim, handled my bags and offered me a copy of the
New York Times. I slid into the backseat. The soft leather
cushions felt great after flying all night in coach. I forced my
tired eyes to focus on the front page of the *Times.* Hostages
taken in Bolivia. An embassy bombing in Sri Lanka. Flooding
in Texas. So this was all the news that's fit to print?

I looked up from my paper. Our limo had already left the expressway and was cruising down a surface road in an industrial area. Old warehouses lined the worn asphalt street. At an intersection, I looked to the right and saw Lower Manhattan stationed across the Hudson River. That meant we were still in New Jersey, heading north into Hoboken—or maybe Union City.

"Excuse me, Salim. Where are we going?" I asked.

"Don't worry, Mr. Marrow. I take you to the right place," he said.

My heart skipped a beat. Was I in danger? I had assumed that Salim was sent by Isaac Kassif. What if he was working for someone else? Could Benson's crackpot murder theory be true?

My logical mind reasserted itself. *Don't panic. You're sleep deprived. You've been watching too many spy movies. Besides, why would someone want to harm you? You're a writer, not James Bond. You know nothing.*

I began watching street signs, trying to keep track of my location. After a few more blocks, the limo pulled into one of the warehouses, a three-story red brick structure that had probably stood since the late 1800s. The building's facade still bore the faint outlines of an old liniment ad painted a century ago. A motorized door shut behind us.

Inside the warehouse I saw a twelve-foot ceiling of massive wooden timbers joined by cast-iron plates. The ground floor was well lit with modern fluorescent tubes. Salim stopped the car and turned to me. "Wait here, Mr. Marrow." He took the keys and disappeared.

By now I was very concerned. I thought I might be in trouble, but I wasn't sure. I tried opening the limo door; it swung freely. Salim had made no effort to conceal our location from me. I still had my cell phone; I turned it on and got a strong signal. I could call 911, but what would I tell them? I *might* have been kidnapped?

I decided to phone my wife and tell her where I was. If I was abducted or killed, at least the police would have something to go on. It was still early in Alaska, so the call went straight to voice mail. I waited impatiently for the beep. "Honey, this is David. Don't panic, but some strange stuff is going on here. I was picked up at Newark Airport by a limo, driven by a man named Salim. Wait a minute . . ."

I jumped out of the car and ran around to the back. "The license plate is New York number BNE9473. We are in a warehouse near the corner of Twelfth and Shipyard Lane. I think we're in Hoboken, New Jersey. Call me back as soon as you get this message. If I don't answer, then give this information to the police in Newark. I hope this is nothing. I love you with all my heart. Bye."

I was contemplating my next move when a metal door opened to my right. Out of the doorway strode a heavyset man. Curled locks of dark brown hair drooped from under a snap-brimmed hat. The man was a textbook Orthodox Jew, dressed head to toe in black. He had a broad smile and a prominent gap between his front teeth.

"Mr. Murrow, thank you for coming. I am Isaac," the man said. He approached me and offered his hand.

"This is not what I expected," I said, looking around the warehouse.

"I apologize. One cannot be too careful these days. Would you like to have something to eat?"

"Yes, I'm starved. I'm guessing it will be kosher?"

Isaac let out a hearty laugh. "Of course. Salim?" The driver opened the front passenger door of the limo and produced a pair of brown-bag lunches. Placing a hand on my back, Isaac led me through a small empty office and out the front door, onto the street.

Isaac pointed back at the building. "This warehouse belongs to a friend. He said it was a good place for us to meet. The hotel, not so good." He looked up and down the street and then continued walking. "How long have you known Father Spiro?"

"I didn't know him at all. He died the night before I went to meet him," I said.

Isaac looked surprised. "I am meeting with you out of respect for Father Spiro. People in my position are expected to limit our contact with Gentiles. This is a rule I break often," he said with another broad smile. I liked this man already.

We carried our brown bags down to the waterfront. Kassif led us to a pocket park with an empty bench and a beautiful view of Midtown Manhattan and the Hudson River. The July sun felt good on my tired shoulders. I unwrapped my sandwich—corned beef on rye. It was my favorite. *How did he know?*

Between bites, Isaac Kassif explained that he was a Hebrew scholar from Jerusalem and an expert in ancient Hebrew dialects. He had met Father Spiro in the 1970s during one of his many trips to Israel. The two developed a friendship and had corresponded over the years.

Isaac described himself as an ecumenical Orthodox Jew. "I have always had great respect for Christians," he said. "I don't care what some say about you."

I thanked him on behalf of all Christians. Then I asked, "Why did you bring me here? Why didn't we just talk by phone or e-mail?"

"I belong to a very orthodox group," he said. "They strongly discourage contact with outsiders, particularly high-profile leaders of other religions. We're not even supposed to mix with Conservative or Reform Jews. Our mail, telephone calls, and e-mail are monitored. I had this trip planned, so I decided to meet you while I was in the USA. And it made sense to meet here in New Jersey instead of Manhattan. Less noticeable."

Isaac fumbled with a bag of pretzels. "About a year ago, I came under pressure to cut off all contact with Father Spiro and his friend Benson. When your message came in, some were upset. That's why I answered you by postal letter and asked you not to e-mail me again."

Kassif paused to nosh on a pretzel and then continued. "Now let me tell you why we are here. Years ago, Father Spiro gave me two documents. One was written in an obscure dialect of Hebrew. This tongue died out in about the sixth century and was only spoken by a small group of Jews who lived on the Mediterranean coast. The second document was written in Nabataean, an Aramaic dialect with similarly ancient roots.

"Spiro asked me to translate the documents. I worked for months. It was very difficult. The Hebrew dialect was unfamiliar and a challenge to decipher. The Nabataean was even harder. Sentences would begin and end in midthought. It was almost as if I was translating a document that had been burned in a fire, and all I had to work with were the scraps of paper that survived—do you see what I mean?"

I nodded and chewed as Kassif continued his story. "The script was also strange. The manuscripts were obviously copied by a hand that did not know Hebrew or Aramaic well. A few of the characters were misdrawn. It took me hundreds of hours to interpret them. It turned out to be one of the most difficult translations of my life."

"Were you able to figure out what the documents said?"

"As I told you, I had only part of the documents, so the writings lacked context. But they were obviously written by the same person and were probably parts of a single work."

Isaac dug out another pretzel but then stopped and turned to face me. "David, these ancient documents referred to a map—a map that leads men to life."

As Isaac said the word *map* I briefly choked on my sandwich. *He's talking about Spiro's map*, I thought. *Maybe it does exist.* I looked at Kassif. His dark eyes were locked on mine, trying to read my emotions. I felt the need to conceal my surprise. "Tell me about this map," I said, with a nonchalance that was not quite believable.

Kassif continued. "The author claimed that any man who follows this map will unlock vast spiritual power. This map was followed by all the great men of the Tanakh, or what you would call the Old Testament."

"Which men are you speaking of?" I asked.

"Abraham, Moses, Elijah, David. These were some of the names I translated. Since I was working with partial manuscripts, there may be others mentioned in the sections I did not possess."

Good heavens, I thought. *A map that was known to the patriarchs? If it exists, it could be the archaeological find of the ages.*

Isaac continued, "The author's chronology was strange. For example, he referred to Levi and Joshua as contemporaries, even though they lived centuries apart."

"What do you mean?" I asked.

"Levi was said to be the keeper of the map. The manuscript said that Joshua gave the map to Levi, and Levi hid it with his scroll. How could this be? Levi was one of the twelve sons of Jacob, and he died centuries before Joshua. And what is 'Levi's scroll'? As far as we know, Levi left no writings."

I felt the rush of pleasure Sherlock Holmes gets the moment he cracks a case. "You're assuming that your documents were written by a Jew," I said. "What if they were written by a Christian?"

Kassif lifted his brow. "What are you saying?"

"The name Joshua can also be rendered as *Yeshua*. As you know, that's the Hebrew name for *Jesus*. And Jesus had a disciple named Matthew, who was also known as Levi. Your document is probably claiming that Jesus gave the map to Matthew, who hid it among his writings."

The revelation fell on Kassif like a summer thunderstorm. "Of course!" he exclaimed, clapping his hands together in delight. "This must be the answer."

My phone rang. It was my wife. I excused myself, stepped away, and answered the call. It took about five minutes to convince her that my body was not floating down the Hudson River. After a half dozen "I love yous" and a promise to call her back as soon as I was done talking with Isaac, I was able to return to the park bench. The Hebrew scholar was just finishing his sandwich. I apologized for the interruption, and Kassif picked up his story.

"Once my translation was done, I handed it over to Spiro. I asked him where he got the documents. He refused to tell me. I asked if other sections might still exist. Again he declined, saying he was sworn to secrecy."

"What do you know about this map?" I asked.

"Nothing," Kassif said. "I was hoping you had gleaned some knowledge of it during your time in the U.K. Unfortunately, you never met Spiro. What about this other man? Spiro's assistant?"

"Benson? He mentioned the map, but he didn't seem to know anything about it," I said. "He gave me your e-mail address."

A distant tugboat sounded its horn. Isaac stared across the Hudson River. Besides a few seagulls, we were the only creatures in the park. Kassif turned toward me and spoke. "You may wonder why I asked you to come. Let me speak very plainly. I want you to help me find the rest of this document so I can finish the translation. I gave a year of my life to this project—I don't want to go to my grave with this riddle unsolved. And consider the possibilities! If you help uncover an early Christian work, think of what it might mean for your religion—and for your reputation as an author."

A combination of wonder, ego, jet lag, caffeine, and lack of sleep had my head spinning. I was too tired to strategize, so I finally just told the truth. "Isaac, I know nothing about the map other than what I've told you. And I don't know anything about your manuscript other than what you just told me. I'm just a writer from Alaska, not an archaeologist or a linguist."

"But neither are you a member of my sect. You can interact freely. Ask questions." Then he added with a sigh, "You can send and receive e-mail."

I smiled and shook my head. "Isaac, I'm afraid you brought me all this way for nothing."

"Nonsense!" he exclaimed. "It seems you have solved the identity of Levi. Soon you will have me reading the New Testament." Isaac chuckled at his own little joke.

"If I do learn something, how can I reach you?" I asked.

"Don't worry. I'll contact you from time to time. This is how it must be."

With that, Isaac sprang to his feet and began walking briskly back to the warehouse. I had to trot to keep up with him. The Hebrew scholar led me back through the office door and into the bay where Salim was waiting. Isaac spoke quickly to the driver in a language I did not understand. He turned to me and said, "Salim will take you to your hotel. Do you like the theater?"

"I love it," I said.

"Good. Speak to the concierge, and he will get you a ticket to whichever show you want to see—simply charge it to your room. Then tomorrow you can be a tourist. Salim will collect your bags in the morning at the hotel while you're out sightseeing. Call him on his mobile phone, and he'll pick you up wherever you happen to be and take you back to the airport in time for your flight."

"That's very kind of you." I approached Kassif to shake his hand, but he lifted a palm and spoke with an ominous tone. "Mr. Murrow, my people have a saying: 'He who overturns a stone should expect to find a scorpion.' Truth always has opponents. You should be very careful as you search for this map."

Instead of a glitzy Broadway show, I chose to watch a chatty one-act play at the Second Stage Theatre on West Forty-third. That was a mistake. I was so tired I must have fallen asleep during the performance, which seemed to last about twenty minutes.

I walked back to the hotel and got ready for bed. But thanks to my seventy-one-dollar catnap (the face value of the ticket), I was now fully awake. The clock read midnight, but my body was still on Alaska time, and my mind was raring to go.

After an hour of insomnia, I flipped on the light, pulled a paperback New Testament from my briefcase, and started studying Levi's scroll, aka the gospel of Matthew. I was so engrossed in the text that I did not notice a small object that was pushed under the door of my hotel room.

Chapter 4

GREEK TO ME

The Manhattan hotel room was quiet and comfortable. I was finally enjoying a deep, restful sleep. But I was about to be awakened by a silent intruder.

Before going to bed, I had pulled the blackout curtains closed, but a tiny gap less than a centimeter wide remained. As the sun rose over Manhattan, a shaft of light traveled across my chest, neck, and face and then hit me in the eyes. *Good morning!*

I looked at the clock: 6:42 a.m. I'd gotten about four hours of sleep, to go with the two hours of sitting-straight-up airplane shut-eye the night before. I lay in bed for fifteen minutes trying to return to dreamland, but it was no use.

Ugh. I felt my way to the bathroom, hoping a hot shower would get my blood pumping. My flight didn't leave Newark until 5:40 p.m., so I had most of the day free to see some sights.

After shaving and showering, I stepped out of the bathroom and found three items on the floor by the door: my room receipt, a copy of *USA Today*, and a plain manila envelope. I opened it and found a handwritten note:

Dear Mr. Murrow,

There is a monk named Gerasimos who lives in the Pankronos monastery in the region of Mount Athos in Greece. He may possess the answer we both seek. Please visit him right away.

If you are unable to make this journey, please return the accompanying documents to your driver and enjoy a pleasant trip home.

K.

The envelope contained six documents: a visa to enter Greece, bearing my name and passport number; another document written completely in Greek, bearing stamps and signatures; a bus ticket; a ferry pass; a hotel reservation in the city of Ouranoupolis; and a round-trip business-class ticket from Newark to Thessaloniki, with a stop in Athens. The flight was scheduled to depart tonight at 5:30 and would return me to Anchorage six days later. The ticket's face value was $15,389.

I stood there, wrapped in a towel, stunned. Questions raced into my brain: *Who is funding this adventure? How did they get my passport number? Am I in danger? People don't throw around this kind of money unless they want something. Should I even consider doing this?*

I glanced at the clock. It was 7:55 a.m.—or 3:55 a.m. in Alaska. It would be at least three hours before I could call my wife and friends for advice. I flipped open the laptop to check my calendar. I had some appointments over the next week, but nothing I couldn't reschedule.

I went online and looked up the Pankronos monastery. It was located in a semi-autonomous region of Greece known as Mount Athos, a peninsula jutting into the Aegean

Sea. The peninsula is sometimes referred to as the Greek Orthodox Vatican, under Greek rule but controlled by the church. Mount Athos is home to twenty monasteries, a few farms, dense forests, and not much else. Two daily ferries provide the only access to the peninsula. Women are prohibited from setting foot on its lands.

The online photos of the monastery were breathtaking. Pankronos was perched high on a cliff overlooking the rugged Aegean coastline. The monastery looked like an extension of the cliff itself, seeming to have grown straight out of the rock face. I began e-mailing these pages to my wife, along with a message explaining all that had happened since we last talked.

She called about ten thirty Eastern time. She had gotten my e-mail. I expected her to be rattled, especially after the way I'd frightened her the day before. But her amazing bravery stepped forward again. "You're halfway around the world already; why not go to Greece?" She warned me to stay away from the Greek women and was relieved to hear that females are barred from Mount Athos.

I warned her that I would be out of communication for five days. My cell phone provider offered no service in Greece, and there were no telephones or Internet in the monastic region. My wife's response was amazing. "David, you've been wanting more adventure in your life. Go!" We prayed together for wisdom, faith, and protection. Then she released me into the care of God.

Instead of spending my New York afternoon sightseeing, I marched up and down Broadway, buying clothing and a large duffel bag for the trip to Greece. (I had brought only enough clothes for two days.) Salim picked me up at Macy's at two o'clock, and we were in the Holland Tunnel, headed for the Newark Airport by two thirty.

It's not easy to get to Mount Athos. The flight to Athens took eleven hours, and the hop to Thessaloniki burned another two. From there I transferred to a bus that carried me to the port city of Ouranoupolis. I arrived about an hour before sunset. My hotel was just four short blocks from the bus station, but the heat and my fatigue made the walk feel like a mile. I skipped dinner and went to bed at six thirty. I slept thirteen hours straight.

My room tab included a breakfast of olives, bread, and cheese. It was like nothing I'd ever eaten, and I devoured every morsel. I arrived at the dock at eight thirty and had my travel permit checked at the Pilgrims Office (this was the document written completely in Greek). The guard said I was allowed to stay on the island for four days. If I overstayed or took any religious artifacts off the peninsula, I would face stiff fines or even jail. I stepped aboard the ferry at eight forty-five, and we were under way just before nine. The ferry was small, and I counted about thirty-five pilgrims aboard.

The sea crossing was unspeakably pleasant. The ocean was calm; the sun was warm, and the sea breeze cool. Chalky-white cliffs rose out of the surf like proud horses, crowned with manes of green scrub. Seabirds gave chase as we plied the sapphire waters of the Aegean. We passed two monasteries along the way: one attached to a cliffside, and the other tucked into a stone canyon near sea level. I saw no one in the monasteries, nor was there a single fishing boat in the sea.

After about forty-five minutes, our ferry docked at the tiny village of Daphne. A pair of aging minibuses waited to take passengers north to Karyes (the capital) or south toward the peak that gives Mount Athos its name. I boarded the bus headed south.

After several stops at other monasteries, the bus pulled

up at a weathered archway that read *Pankronos*. Four of us got off there. I tipped the driver, grabbed my bags, and walked through the morning heat toward the monastery's gate. My fellow travelers chatted eagerly among themselves in Greek.

The monastery's massive outer doors were sitting open. Inside I found a shaded courtyard with comfortable benches where pilgrims could wait to enter the facility. The courtyard was festooned with flowers, vines, trellises, and . . . *Benson?*

"Mr. Murrow! What a surprise. It's good to see you again." The priest stood and pumped my right hand, practically taking it off my body. He was wearing a plaid, short-sleeved shirt that stretched unwillingly across his barrel chest.

It took me a moment to recover my speech. "Benson, what are you doing here?"

"I'm here to see Gerasimos. How about you?"

"Me too. Did you know I was coming?"

"I suspected you might come. But I didn't know when."

Benson and I sat down on a bench under a shady pergola covered in greenery that was bursting with red blossoms. "How long have you been here?" I asked.

"I arrived on yesterday morning's ferry. This is my second day waiting to see Gerasimos. He's said to be in prayer."

"When will he be out of prayer?" I asked.

"When Gerasimos is ready to see us, that monk will let us in." Benson gestured toward a smallish man in his late forties. The monk was sitting at a desk, blocking a wooden entrance door. He was wearing a black cap and cassock. The top of the cap was like a wide saucer, while the lower part fit snugly around his temples. He was writing in a parchment book with a feather quill. I thought, *What else would a monk be doing?*

I walked up to the monk and introduced myself, telling him I was here to see Gerasimos. He answered me in

accented English, "Gerasimos is in prayer. When he is finished, he will see you. Please, take a seat." His speech was
robotic, and I could barely see lips moving beneath his thick,
salt-and-pepper beard.

Benson and I used our waiting time to get caught up. He
went first. After Father Spiro's death, he had spent about two
weeks pressing for an autopsy but was unable to convince the
coroner it was necessary. "All my other leads turned into dead
ends. Then about a month after we parted, I was contacted
by a man named Yusef, a Muslim who works in Jerusalem,"
Benson said. "He told me about Gerasimos and this monastery. Yusef asked me to be ready to travel here at a moment's
notice. So I waited . . . more than three months, bags packed.
Finally, the call came four days ago. I took the same trip you
did—air, land, and sea—only I arrived a day earlier."

I marveled at our interfaith troupe: an evangelical
Christian, an Anglican priest, an Orthodox Jew, a Muslim,
and now a Greek Orthodox monk. All on the same team—or
so I hoped.

The inner door to the monastery opened, and the three
Greek pilgrims who had ridden on the bus with me were
ushered inside. Benson and I remained seated and continued talking. I apologized for waiting so long to contact Isaac
Kassif. I told Benson about our strange meeting in New Jersey,
just three days ago, although it felt like another lifetime. The
priest was transfixed as I shared what I had learned about the
map, the patriarchs, and the connection to Levi (Matthew).
"This ticks a few boxes for me," Benson said. "Spiro was very
tight-lipped on details."

I asked Benson, "What about this phrase—'Jesus gave
the map to Levi, who hid it with his scroll'? Any idea what
it means?"

"I don't know," he said. "Perhaps the answer lies behind that door."

The afternoon passed with no sign of Brother Gerasimos. The courtyard was shaded, but the thick walls trapped heat. About once every half hour, I checked with the monk at the door, but his answer was always the same: "Gerasimos is in prayer. When he is finished, he will see you. Please, take a seat."

By three thirty, my stomach was growling like a cornered dog—so loudly that Benson heard it. The priest pulled a cake of pressed figs from his daypack and shared it with me, along with a little wine from a flask. Greece is a strange country— it's easier to get bad wine than good drinking water.

As we were finishing our snack, the monastery door opened, and a gardener emerged with two large watering cans. He worked his way around the courtyard, giving each plant the proper ration of life-giving liquid. When he got near us, he stopped and stared. To my surprise, he addressed us in English. "Which one of you is the American?"

"I am," I answered.

"What is your business here?" the gardener asked in a challenging tone.

I looked at Benson. Then I spoke. "We are here on a matter of some importance."

"That's it with you Americans, always doing something important," the gardener said. His English was flawless. I had been warned that some Greeks harbored anti-American attitudes, but this was the first time I'd personally encountered such outright hostility.

"I beg your pardon?" I asked with ample resentment.

"Let me ask you a simple question. Are you men disciples of Jesus?"

Again I looked at Benson. He remained silent. "Yes, of course," I answered.

The gardener lowered his watering cans and stooped to our level. "You do not know what a disciple is. The brothers in this monastery have given every drachma they have to the poor. They practice self-denial. Tell me, what pleasure have you denied yourself lately? How many televisions, computers, and telephones do you have? How many cars? Homes? Bank accounts? Do you enjoy the companionship of a woman?"

My fight instinct took over. "Are you out of your mind? What are you talking about?"

The gardener's green eyes flashed with indignation. He picked up a fig that I had carelessly dropped on the ground. "You are so weak you cannot even wait a few hours without filling your stomach." He pointed at the monk sitting by the door. "You pester Brother Antipos every few minutes because your time is valuable. You want results and you want them now."

"I'm here to see Gerasimos, not to get a lecture from you!" A cocktail of rage and indignation surged through my body. My face was flushed. My hands involuntarily contracted into fists.

The gardener wasn't done: "Christ said, 'If you want to be great, be a servant.' Who are you serving? When have you given, not expecting a return? Men like you make God want to vomit!"

The gardener stood and picked up his cans. I jumped to my feet and blocked his way. "Gerasimos will hear about your rude treatment of his guests. What is your name?"

The gardener stared at me. His eyes were now burning coals. "My name? You know my name."

He turned and walked toward the door. Benson lurched

past me and grabbed the gardener by the arm before he could disappear. I heard Benson muttering what sounded like apologies. The gardener listened, looked to the sky, and then whispered something into Benson's ear. He and his watering cans passed through the doorway and vanished into the monastery.

Benson wheeled around and grabbed me by the arm with surprising force. He said, "You fool! That was Gerasimos."

Chapter 5

LESSONS

Pankronos monastery is twenty-five kilometers from the nearest town, and the last minibus had already left for the night. The sun was setting, and Benson and I were stranded. Our only option for food and lodging lay seventy meters straight down a cliff. Tucked in a protected cove, a Greek fisherman lived in a tiny home overlooking a tranquil bay. He ran a lucrative business taking in stranded pilgrims. For fifty-five euros a night, his guests received a simple seafood dinner, a light breakfast, and a place to sleep on the deck of his fishing boat, which he anchored some fifty meters offshore. For an extra five euros, the skipper would pack the pilgrim a lunch. No reservations needed.

Benson and I walked down the narrow path to the anchorage, zigging and zagging as it wound its way down the cliff. Sunlight danced off the face of the ocean, and a cool sea breeze offered relief. But Benson was still red hot.

"You almost ruined everything," he said. "These are monks, men who have left everything to follow Christ. The very foundation of their faith is self-control—something you showed little of today."

I didn't know what to say.

"The Orthodox have a more comprehensive view of Christ than we do in the West," Benson said. "Jesus would always test men with sharp words. When he encountered hypocrisy, he did not hold back. Why should you be surprised when a fellow Christian points out your weaknesses? You should have responded with humility, not self justification."

Benson huffed and puffed as we picked our way down the rocky trail. His fury continued. "In the West, we think that 'being like Jesus' means always nice and polite. Think back over all the years you've been a Christian. Has another believer ever treated you the way Gerasimos did today?"

I searched my memory. "No, I've never been spoken to like that by another Christian."

"Yet that's exactly how Jesus spoke to the Pharisees—men he loved. You finally experienced what it's like to stand in the presence of a righteous God. Gerasimos offered you a gift, and you threw it back in his face."

The weight of my foolishness sat like a grindstone on my chest. It was my first encounter with the Lion of Judah, and I had failed miserably.

"When you whispered to Gerasimos, what did you say?" I asked sheepishly.

"I apologized on your behalf. I asked him to meet with us tomorrow."

"And he said . . . ?"

"He questioned whether we were true disciples of Jesus," Benson said. "But he said he would pray about seeing us tomorrow. Gerasimos possesses a powerful secret—one that must not fall into the hands of an enemy. He needs to be certain that we are allies."

By now we were at the water's edge. The fisherman smiled when he saw Benson, who had lodged here the previous night. Our host was probably in his early sixties yet still muscular, dressed in a dirty white T-shirt, rain slicker pants, and boots. His lips held a cigarette above a chin that looked to be three days past its last shave. He was standing on a tiny beachhead of broken rock, roasting an unknown flatfish over hot coals. He reached into his pocket and handed me a laminated pamphlet written in four languages. It explained the rates and policies of his "boat and breakfast."

Minutes later, the three of us gathered in his cramped cottage to enjoy a simple meal of fish, bread, olives, potatoes, and, of course, more cheap wine. We were his only guests that night. After supper we helped with the dishes, washed up, and climbed into a small dinghy. The incoming tide had already covered the small beach where our dinner was cooked. The waves had extinguished the fire and carried the coals out to sea. The fisherman rowed us out to his boat as the last rays of light expired in the western sky.

Our host spread thin cotton sleeping pads and pillows on the deck. He produced a pair of worn wool blankets that looked to be military surplus. Then he showed us where the life jackets and tarps were stored in case of bad weather. He turned out the electric lights on the boat and rowed the dinghy back to shore.

Benson and I lay on our backs, the sky above us awash in stars. Their beauty immediately moved me to prayer. I begged God to forgive my foolishness and to give us a second chance with Gerasimos. Up to this point I'd reserved a healthy skepticism about our mission, but in that moment I fully committed myself. Isaac's words rang in my mind: *"Any man who follows this map will unlock vast spiritual power."* I wanted to find that map—not only to share it with others, but also because I needed to follow it myself.

At my side I could hear Benson reciting liturgical prayers under his breath. The gentle rocking of the boat quickly lulled us into a deep slumber.

———————————

The fisherman and his cigarette arrived just after dawn to take us back to shore. After another unusual olive-based breakfast, Benson and I arrived at the monastery around seven thirty. The outer doors were open, and a different monk was playing security guard. This one was much older and spoke no English. We asked for Gerasimos, but I wasn't sure if he understood.

Benson and I spent the morning learning more about each other. I told him about my life in Alaska, my conversion from a television producer to an author, and the rapid growth of Church for Men.

Then Benson regaled me for hours with stories of his youth. At one time he had been a skilled rugby player, but an injury at age twenty cut his athletic career short. He joined the Royal Air Force at twenty-one and spent eight years in active duty. Then it was off to seminary and the priesthood. He was married at thirty and widowed at forty. He never remarried. Then Benson told me of his love for fishing, which led to several rounds of competitive boasting (he now knows better than to swap fish stories with an Alaskan).

Five Greek pilgrims arrived around eleven thirty and were immediately ushered into the monastery. Around noon Benson and I stepped outside into the sun and shared a simple lunch of dried fish, bread, and an orange.

The afternoon passed slowly. I dozed off a couple of times, waking up with cotton mouth. At precisely 4:00 p.m., the door opened, and the five pilgrims emerged from the monastery.

The minibus would arrive soon to take them back to the ferry. Benson and I talked about going with them to Karyes, which had a small hotel with proper beds and showers. After many hours in the Aegean heat, we were both in need of a good scrubbing.

As we were deliberating, a monk strode through the door. He was a tall man who looked even taller in his chimney pot hat. He looked to be in his late fifties, with wavy white hair and a trim beard. He had a bony face with high cheekbones, a prominent brow, and penetrating green eyes. He radiated strength, calm, and power.

It was Gerasimos, but this time he looked the part. Dressed head to toe in black, the humble gardener had been transformed into an ambassador of the King. Benson and I both stood. "Welcome to Pankronos, gentlemen," he said.

Benson took his right hand. Then he offered his left to me. The moment he touched me, words of contrition flowed. "Gerasimos, I am so sorry about yesterday," I said. "Will you forgive me?"

"Do not apologize with your words, but with your actions." His eyes bored through my soul. Then he said, "Come."

He led us outside and down the path toward the fisherman's hut. Gerasimos's pace was slow and deliberate. "David, I was up at dawn, praying for you."

I knew better than to speak.

The monk continued, "The Spirit of Jesus assured me that you are a true disciple who is on his second journey. However, yesterday you forgot the lessons of your first journey. This happens from time to time. I prayed for you, and the Lord has forgiven you."

My Western pride stiffened at these words. *Who is he to tell me I'm forgiven?* But then I remembered the Pharisees' indignation when Jesus offered a similar absolution to a desperate man. I quieted my heart and received the grace of God.

Benson finally spoke. "Gerasimos, what do you mean by first journey and second journey?"

"Tomorrow I will teach you the three journeys of Jesus. Then your eyes will be opened and you will find what you came for." The monk stopped. "I finish the morning Orthros at eight. We will meet in the courtyard at eight thirty. I will provide food and drink for the day. Good evening, gentlemen."

With that, Gerasimos began walking back toward the monastery. If we were to meet him at eight thirty, the hotel in Karyes was out of the question. We would have to spend another night on the fishing boat.

Benson and I continued down the path. My thoughts wandered: *The three journeys of Jesus? What is he talking about? Well, at least he's agreed to see us.*

My third day on Athos dawned just like the others: sunny and clear. In fact, I had not seen a cloud since arriving in Greece.

Benson and I waited in the courtyard for Gerasimos to appear. Another day—another monk was guarding the inner door. This one spoke very good British English, and we passed a few pleasant minutes chatting with him about monastic life.

To our surprise, Gerasimos did not enter the courtyard from the monastery door, but walked in from outside the compound. "Good morning. Would you gentlemen come with me?" He was dressed in a simpler cassock, and his chimney pot hat was gone. We followed him up to the road, where

a brown 1989 Fiat sedan sat parked under the arch. The three of us got into the car, with Gerasimos taking the wheel.

"Is this your car?" I asked.

"No, our community maintains two cars and a truck. This car is used mainly by the abbot. He gave me permission to use it today, for your instruction."

Benson spoke from the backseat. "Gerasimos, how is it that you speak such good English, with an American accent?"

"I am a dual Greek-American citizen," the monk said. "I lived in Connecticut until I was fifteen years old. Then my family moved back to Greece. My father was in shipping. I learned English from Jack Paar, Milton Berle, and Captain Kangaroo." I smiled at the cultural references; the Briton didn't know what Gerasimos was talking about.

The monk pulled a compass from his pocket and handed it to me. "David, we are headed to Mount Athos, which is southeast of here. Please let me know if we are traveling in the right direction." Gerasimos put the Fiat into gear, and we began climbing a steep hill.

I held the compass as steady as I could. The device indicated that we were driving northwest. "It looks like we are headed away from the mountain," I said.

The monk glanced at the compass. "Indeed we are. But just wait a moment."

About five hundred meters up the hill, a hairpin turn took us hard to the right. The compass needle pivoted with it. "Now we're headed in the right direction," I said.

"David, let me ask you a question. When I left the monastery, why didn't I drive immediately toward the mountain?"

"We had to follow the road," I said.

"And what if I had insisted on driving directly toward the summit?"

"We would have plunged off a cliff into the sea."

About that time we encountered another hairpin turn. The car and the compass needle swung to the northwest again.

Gerasimos continued, "We are headed the wrong direction once more. Now, receive this lesson: The first journey of Jesus moves a man away from the direction he wants to go. The second journey of Jesus moves him toward it. The third journey moves him away from it again."

I had no idea what Gerasimos was talking about, but I absorbed his words. Perhaps this riddle would lead us to the map.

———

After a while, we broke out of the hills into a level clearing. Some men were training horses in a makeshift corral. Gerasimos pulled over, got out of the car, and invited us to sit with him on an ancient stone wall.

"Benson, have you ever worked with horses?"

"No, but I was around them a bit as a boy," the vicar said.

"Do you see that colt? Soon the time will come to train it. What's the first thing these cowboys will do?"

"They'll have to break the colt," Benson said.

"Yes, and once the colt is broken, then what?" the monk asked.

"They will train it to work," Benson said.

"Right again. Now, after many years of faithful service, what will they do with the horse?"

Benson paused. "Put him out to pasture?"

"Perhaps, but a very successful horse will spend its old age as a stud. This is how cowboys preserve the spirit of a good horse even after it dies. It lives on in the next generation

of horses," Gerasimos said. "So this is the second lesson: the first journey of Jesus is like breaking the horse, the second is like working the horse, and the third is like sending the horse out to reproduce."

Benson and I shared a quick glance, still not understanding what the monk was trying to teach us. Before we could puzzle over the meaning of the parable, Gerasimos led us across the road and through a stand of trees, where an abandoned building stood. We walked through a doorway without a door, into a dark chamber filled with dirt and cobwebs. The roof was made of wooden planks and seemed to be one thunderstorm away from falling in on itself.

School was in session. "Tell me, Benson, how was this building formed?"

"I don't know what you mean, Gerasimos."

"What came first? The roof, the walls . . . ?"

"No, Teacher. The foundation came first, then the walls, then the roof."

"And so it is with the three journeys. The first journey is merely the foundation. It's largely invisible, but it upholds the entire building. The second journey is the structure. This is the part of the building that is seen and appreciated by all. The third journey is the roof, which completes the structure and protects the inhabitants. This is your third lesson."

Back on the road, we caught our first glimpse of Mount Athos. It was a beautiful peak, gleaming white in the hot July sun. "David, tell me about your journey from America. Where did you stop?" Gerasimos asked.

"First, I flew from New York to Athens. Then I changed

planes and flew to Thessaloniki. From there I took a bus to Ouranoupolis, and finally the ferry to Daphne."

Gerasimos made his point: "New York is a city of tens of millions. Athens is a city of millions. Thessaloniki is a city of thousands. Ouranoupolis is a city of hundreds. Daphne is a city of tens. So now you have your fourth lesson: on each leg of your journey, you will find fewer and fewer people; the farther you go, the more alone you will be."

About one o'clock, we reached the end of the road. The mountain was close now, and the terrain ahead was steep. The surrounding lands were heavily wooded. Gerasimos parked the car and fetched a blanket and box from the trunk. The three of us enjoyed a pleasant lunch under the welcoming shade of a giant chestnut tree.

"Tell me about this tree, David. How did it begin?" Gerasimos asked.

Instead of answering his question, I jumped and grabbed a low-hanging branch, tearing off a still-green chestnut. I handed it to the monk without saying a word.

"Correct," Gerasimos said. "Not every seed becomes a tree, but every tree starts as a seed. The best trees grow big and strong, and they provide shelter to the animals— and shade to vagabonds like us." The monk paused to take a drink and then continued. "But one day the tree finds its ultimate fate. It might burn in a fire or fall in a windstorm. Or a human might come along and turn the tree into whatever he chooses. The tree gives its life to become a home for man, or to provide light and heat for cooking. It might also become a book or a chair or a fine musical instrument. So this is the fifth lesson: The first journey is like the seed, and the second is like the tree. The third journey is not fulfilled until the tree is sacrificed."

Benson and I contemplated the lessons as we finished our lunch. What an opportunity this was—wandering the Greek countryside, absorbing parables created just for us. It was almost like sitting at the feet of Christ.

I still had not asked Gerasimos about the map directly. I tried to bring up the subject four or five times, but the words simply would not form on my lips. My heart told me that this was a time to listen—to feast on whatever this remarkable teacher chose to serve us.

After lunch the three of us stretched out on the ground. Sleep came quickly and naturally. When I awoke, Gerasimos was loading the car. "Come with me before the ants carry you away," he said with a lifted eyebrow and the smallest of grins. It was the first time I'd seen him smile.

It was after three o'clock when we got back under way. The well-maintained Fiat purred contentedly as it carried us back to the monastery. We traveled through dense forests that had never seen an ax blade. The lush deciduous trees reminded me of the eastern United States. "When is the last time you were in Connecticut?" I asked Gerasimos.

"I visited an aunt there a few summers ago. The trees reminded me very much of Mount Athos—Hold on!" Without warning, Gerasimos slammed on the brakes and swerved onto a side road. The narrow trail curved quickly to the left, hiding us from view of the highway. The monk swung the front of the car toward the main road, fishtailing the rear end in the process. I thought, *How did a monk learn to drive like this?* Gerasimos killed the engine and peered through the trees. "Be quiet," he said.

A few seconds later a black Mercedes sedan motored past

us on the highway. It appeared to be carrying two men, but it was hard to tell looking through thick foliage. The vehicle kept driving and disappeared around a curve. There was no indication that we had been seen.

"That car has been following us," said the monk. "It's been hanging back, trying to remain undetected." Gerasimos started the engine and returned to the road. But instead of heading toward the monastery, we drove back in the direction we came, toward the mountain and away from the black sedan. Something about the car clearly unnerved him.

Not five minutes later, things got much worse. The Fiat's engine sputtered and died. We coasted to a stop on the side of the road. Gerasimos looked to the heavens and said something in Greek. I don't think it was a prayer. Then he turned to me and said, "The fuel tank is empty."

Chapter 6

SLUMBER PARTY

Gerasimos was adamant—he would stay with the Fiat while he sent Benson and me for gas. We begged him to go with us, but he refused. He had promised the abbot he would not leave the car. Fortunately, Gerasimos knew a farmer who lived just up the road. He scribbled a note in Greek, asking his friend for a few liters of fuel. The monk gave us a detailed description of the farmhouse and its distinctive flat-roofed barn.

Benson and I set out, our heads on a swivel. We were determined to avoid the Mercedes.

After a thirty-minute walk, we found the property just as Gerasimos had described it. The farmer was a middle-aged man with leathery skin and a pleasant demeanor. He read the note and motioned for us to sit on the porch while he disappeared into an outbuilding. About five minutes later he brought us a battered plastic antifreeze jug full of petrol. We smiled, thanked him in English, and began walking back to the Fiat. The sun had already dropped behind the treetops. Birds and insects were beginning their evensong. The sky would be dark in less than an hour.

We walked for thirty minutes, then thirty-five, then forty.

There was no sign of Gerasimos or the car. "We've gone too far," I said.

"Really?" Benson asked. "Maybe we haven't gone far enough."

"That's impossible," I said. "We've already walked ten minutes longer this direction. I think we passed the spot a while ago."

"All right. Let's think this through," Benson said. "Gerasimos could have found some petrol and gone looking for us, but how could we have missed him?" The priest paused and then whispered, "Maybe the men in the black sedan got him."

"Well, there's nothing we can do for him now," I said. "We need to find a place to spend the night. I don't want to be out on this road after dark."

We decided our best bet was to return to the farmer's house and ask for shelter, even though we knew no Greek and the farmer spoke no English. Fear and uncertainty stalked us as we backtracked. *What if we march right past the farmhouse in the dark? Where will we sleep if the farmer refuses or can't understand our request? Did we misunderstand Gerasimos somehow?*

The drone of an automobile motor jerked me back to reality. I looked behind me. An eerie glow was forming over the crown of the road. I grabbed Benson by the shoulder and pushed him into the shallow ditch. We hit the ground just as a black Mercedes topped the hill. Its ice-blue xenon headlights probed the grass around us. I crouched closer to the ground, silently praying we had not been seen.

The car slowed and then stopped some twenty meters away. I heard a door open, and then a faint clicking noise. Then shoes crunching on gravel. The beam of a flashlight passed over us. Surely we had been spotted. Benson and I did not move.

After a minute, I heard a man saying words I didn't understand. Then a door closed and the Mercedes resumed its travel. "Don't move," I whispered softly. I thought maybe one of our pursuers had stayed behind, crouching in the shadows, waiting for us to show ourselves.

The sky was darkening rapidly, which worked to our advantage. We remained perfectly still for about ten minutes, and then Benson and I began creeping along the ditch. Crickets were chirping, which covered what little noise we were making. My hands and forearms began to bleed, cut by brambles.

After about a hundred meters of belly crawling, I lifted my head and looked back at the road. Best I could tell we were not being pursued, although I couldn't be sure. We got on our hands and knees and crawled another two hundred meters, until the road went around a curve. From there we stood, brushed ourselves off, uttered thanks to God, and continued our journey.

The sky was completely black when we finally arrived at the farmhouse. The farmer looked shocked to see us again—in such a disheveled state, and with no gasoline (I'd left it in the ditch). I did my best to pantomime our story. The farmer looked confused and seemed ready to close the door on us. In desperation, I flopped to the ground and pretended to sleep, complete with snoring. At this, the farmer smiled and invited us into his cottage.

The one-room house was a nineteenth-century bachelor pad. There was nothing tidy about it. There were papers, broken farm tools, animal cages, empty bottles, and horse tack everywhere. To our right stood an ancient woodstove and a simple kitchen, complete with an American-made, hand-operated water pump. In the middle sat a crude table and two chairs. To the left were a bed, a chair, and a wash-basin. The entire house couldn't have been more than fifty square meters.

We had interrupted the man's dinner: a lamb chop and a loaf of bread sat half eaten on the table, along with a bottle of Chianti. The farmer pulled up the extra chair and invited us to sit. He poured us some wine, broke the bread, and gave it to us. He also offered us some jerky, figs, and raw mushrooms. Once dinner was finished, he filled a wine-skin, grabbed a flashlight, and led us outside. He showed us the outhouse and then took us past a chicken coop and into the barn.

The old stone stable had a low ceiling and little ventila-tion. The odor was overpowering at first, but we quickly got used to it. The farmer handed me the wineskin and flash-light, grabbed a pitchfork, and smoothed a pile of hay into a bed. We thanked him again as best we could and settled down for the night. Benson was exhausted after our hike and crawl, and he was snoring before his head hit the hay. I slept fitfully, until that blasted rooster crowed at 4:32 a.m. But you've already heard that part of the story.

We rose just after sunrise. The farmer was gone. We entered his cottage and drew water from the hand pump. Benson and I drank greedily from a tin can. I hadn't had a decent glass of water since arriving in Mount Athos.

Benson and I shared a piece of bread and some jerky. Before we ate, we gave thanks to God for our meager rations and for keeping us safe through the night. We prayed a blessing on the farmer's home and asked protection for Gerasimos. At seven twenty, we set out on foot for the monastery.

The first vehicle to pass us was not a car, but a hay cart drawn by a mule. The driver stopped and made motions for us to hop in. We complied and instantly tripled our speed.

After about twenty minutes, we saw the black Mercedes approaching from the rear. Benson and I quickly buried ourselves in the hay, not sure if we'd been spotted. Within seconds the sedan was on our tail, honking its horn. The cart stopped abruptly. We heard a door open and men speaking insistently in Greek. Benson and I hardly breathed.

We heard the sound of rough wooden clogs scratching on pavement. Moments later someone pulled back our covering. Benson and I stared at two monks—or two men dressed as monks. "Hello," the taller one said. "Come wid us." The man spoke English with a Slavic accent.

"Where?" I asked.

"To Gerasimos. He told us to find you and bring you to Pankronos."

I looked at Benson. He appeared deeply suspicious. If these men had abducted Gerasimos, we were next. Perhaps these were the scorpions Isaac had warned me about.

"Who are you?" I asked.

"I am Brother Pavel, and this is Brother Nikolai. We are from Stravnokita monastery."

"Where is Gerasimos?" Benson asked.

"In Pankronos. We assisted him last night on the road," said Pavel.

I forced a smile. "Thank you for your offer, but we prefer to find our own way back."

The two "monks" looked at each other quizzically. They exchanged a few words in what sounded like Russian. Pavel pointed at the cart driver and said, "Dimitrios goes only two more kilometers. Pankronos is twenty-three kilometers. It is foolish to walk all day in sun and heat."

"We prefer to take our chances," I said. "But thank you."

Again the men looked at each other. This time Nikolai approached me and said, "I want to give you one more chance to come with us." I refused. Benson nodded in agreement.

"Very well," said Pavel with a sigh. "There is a green minibus that passes here about ten o'clock." Pavel waved his arms over his head. "Do this and the driver will pick you up. The bus will take you all the way back to Karyes, and you can ride the afternoon bus to Pankronos if you like—or you can take the blue bus to Daphne and get the ferry. Please remember that you are here on four-day permits, and there are penalties for overstaying. God be with you." To our relief the monks got back into the luxury sedan and sped away. The rickety hay cart began rolling again. Benson looked like a man who had just been spared the gallows.

Now we were thoroughly confused. Were these men really monks trying to help us? Or were they impostors, preparing to abduct us at a time when there were no witnesses? If so, should we go back to the farm? Then a sobering thought struck me: *Four-day permits?* I added it up in my head. *This is my fourth day in Mount Athos. And Benson's fifth.* I pulled my travel documents from a pouch hidden under my shirt. *Nuts!* I thought. *I'm supposed to take the ferry tonight and fly out of Thessaloniki tomorrow afternoon.*

I discussed the situation with Benson. He was aware of the four-day rule. He had planned to ask Gerasimos yesterday if his permit could be extended, but he was so engrossed in figuring out the monk's riddles that he'd completely forgotten. Any extension would have to be authorized by an abbot, and with Gerasimos missing (along with the abbot's car), this was no sure thing.

After twenty minutes, the hay cart dropped us off. We walked down the road nervously, looking for adversaries behind every fence, bush, and tree. We ducked for cover whenever we heard a vehicle approaching. Pure delight flooded our hearts when the minibus approached us from behind, just as Pavel had said. We waved frantically and boarded with relief. In no time we arrived at Karyes. After the isolation of the past three days, this tiny outpost of 225 men felt like a metropolis. Benson and I enjoyed authentic Greek gyros at the hotel café and washed them down with bottled sparkling water.

Our hunger satisfied, Benson and I decided to visit the Pilgrims Office to straighten out the permit situation. The moment the officer saw that Benson had overstayed, he took the priest into custody. We tried to explain what had happened, but the officer's English was limited. Soon another official who spoke no English came and escorted Benson to a concrete building that looked like a lockup. I tried to follow the pair, but the first officer pulled out a nightstick and restrained me. He checked my permit and warned me in broken English that I must leave Mount Athos on the evening ferry or face the same penalty myself.

I left the Pilgrims Office in a daze. *Now what do I do? If I go back to the monastery, I'll overstay my permit and end up in jail tomorrow. I'll miss my flight back to the States for sure.* The voice of reason rang in my mind: *You need to bring this madness to an end. Take the minibus to Daphne now. Get on the evening ferry. You need to get back to your life, your wife and kids. They are depending on you. And there's that passage in Romans about obeying the governmental authorities . . .*

But then another voice whispered: *You can't abandon Benson. If you leave, who will see after him? And what about Gerasimos? You don't know if he's dead or alive. And you can't forget the purpose of your trip: to find the map.*

Then a chilling thought entered my mind. *If Gerasimos was kidnapped or killed, whom will the police suspect? Who were the last two people seen with him?* I pictured myself being detained at the Athens airport—or worse, jailed on suspicion of murder. *Should I make a quick getaway, before the monk's body turns up?*

I'm the type of person who likes to think before making a big decision. I always seek advice. But this time I had the benefit of neither time nor counsel. Options swirled in my head like a rogue tornado. Then a tidbit of Scripture came to mind: "If any of you lacks wisdom, he should ask God." So I sat under a shade tree and prayed. "Lord, I've never lacked as much wisdom as I'm lacking right now. Show me what to do."

Seconds later, a green minibus rumbled up the dusty main street of Karyes. It was bound for the southern end of the peninsula—and Pankronos. Suddenly my path was clear: the answers I sought were at the monastery, and that bus was my only hope of finding them. I jumped up and waved my arms like a man possessed.

Chapter 7

THE FOOL

The minibus left Karyes on time but quickly fell behind schedule. Our driver was a sociable chap who felt the need to stop and spend a few minutes chatting with each passenger who boarded. As the bus idled, it became stiflingly hot, and exhaust crept in the open windows, adding to my anxiety.

We finally reached Pankronos about four thirty. A quartet of happy pilgrims was standing by the roadside, waiting to board. I paid the bus driver, muscled my way through the scrum, and walked quickly toward the massive wooden gates of the monastery. Some clouds were gathering over the ocean. A thin cirrus layer had finally begun to subdue the merciless Greek sun.

I strode into the courtyard and saw a new monk sitting at the desk. This one was a large, strapping fellow. It was his turn to play the role of monastery bouncer, and he looked the part.

"Hello," I said, breathing heavily.

The monk looked startled. He obviously wasn't expecting someone to arrive on the late bus. "English?" he said.

"Yes, I speak English. I'm looking for Gerasimos. Is he here?"

The monk didn't understand. I spoke again: "Gerasimos."

"Gerasimos?" the monk said. He stood and disappeared into the monastery, his broad shoulders barely fitting through the narrow doorway.

Several minutes passed before the door opened again. The burly monk emerged. He smiled and said, "Gerasimos pray." He pointed inside the monastery, leaving no doubt as to the monk's whereabouts.

He's alive and well! Relief flooded my heart, for Gerasimos, and then for myself. *At least I won't be hanged*, I thought.

I turned to the doorman, communicating with a mixture of words and hand gestures. "Can I see Gerasimos?"

The monk nodded and pointed at me. "Yes—you—Gerasimos," he said. Then he gestured for me to sit down.

I walked over to my now-familiar bench. It felt long and empty without my traveling companion at my side. I'd really grown to love the old priest. I had nothing else to do, so I prayed again for his protection.

About forty-five minutes passed. I marveled at how Mount Athos had changed my American sense of time and entitlement. Back in the USA, I'd be summoning the management for an explanation of the delay. But now I sat contentedly, waiting for the monk to appear.

The courtyard was dimming. The sun was now completely blocked by clouds. My watch said 5:32. *In twenty-eight minutes, I will have officially overstayed my permit*, I thought. Ten minutes passed, then twenty. I was getting hungry and thirsty again. Every time I felt a pang, I turned to prayer.

At two minutes until six, the door opened and a monk with a thin face and piercing eyes appeared. "Gerasimos!"

I cried, walking swiftly toward him, taking his outstretched hands. "We were worried about you. Are you all right?"

"Perfectly. Where is Benson?"

"He was detained at the Pilgrims Office. He overstayed his permit," I said with worry in my voice.

"He will be fine. The usual penalty for overstaying one day is 200 euros. The officials probably charged him 250 and kept the rest. This is Greece, after all."

"So what will happen to him now?" I asked.

"I would suppose he is sitting aboard the ferry, waiting to depart for Ouranoupolis, 250 euros poorer."

More relief. My heart lightened. Things were not as bad as I had imagined.

"Gerasimos, what happened last night? We brought the fuel, but you were gone. We thought you might have been kidnapped . . . or worse."

The monk invited me to sit. "First, tell me what you have experienced since we last saw each other," he said.

I launched into a lengthy review: our stay in the farmer's barn, the rooster waking me up, the feeling of being watched, the hay wagon, the strangers in the Mercedes, Benson's detention, and my decision to return to the monastery. I also mentioned the constant prayer that accompanied each experience. The monk sat expressionless as I spoke.

Then it was Gerasimos's turn. "Congratulations, David. You passed the test. I will now reveal the lesson. Yesterday I promised to teach you the three journeys of Jesus. Everything that has happened to you in the past two days has been an illustration of this truth."

I was dumbfounded. I felt my palms beginning to sweat. *A test?*

Gerasimos continued, "Yesterday afternoon, the Fiat truly

did run out of fuel. But that was my plan. The abbot's car is equipped with two fuel tanks, because here on Athos, fuel deliveries can be infrequent. After we encountered the black Mercedes, I switched to the auxiliary tank, knowing it was empty. Within minutes we ran out of fuel. So I sent you and Benson away, switched back to the primary tank, and drove to the monastery. I was home in time for evening prayers.

"About your lodging: I guessed that you would return to the farmer's house. I knew he would put you in the barn because he had no room in his house for guests. This was an important part of your lesson.

"This morning I sent Pavel and Nikolai as another test— to trust or not to trust. I made sure that they warned you about the four-day limit on your permits. This presented you with a choice: Be safe, go back home, and forget about your mission. Or you could take a risk, stay behind, and complete it. Benson's detention was not a part of the plan, but it worked out perfectly."

Blood was pounding in my ears. I was so angry I could have attacked Gerasimos, had it not been for the bouncer monk sitting a few meters away. Before I knew it, my tongue was engaged. "You sick-minded man! You set this whole thing up. You put us through hell. We slept in a barn, sharing our bed with rats. We barely had food. We didn't know if you were dead or alive. And those Russians—we thought they were out to kill us!"

The monk showed no emotion as I leveled the charges. My tirade went on for at least a minute. Finally, Gerasimos looked at me with a strange mixture of judgment and compassion. "Why are you angry? You should be grateful."

"Grateful? For the worst twenty-four hours of my life?"

The monk lowered his voice and fixed his eyes on

mine. "David, remember when we first met? You thought I was a gardener. I asked if you were a disciple of Jesus. Well, now you are, in a way most American believers will never know."

I managed to hold my tongue, so Gerasimos continued: "In the West, you think that study is the key to discipleship. You listen to sermons. You gather in circles and read the Bible. Words go into your brain and are supposed to change your heart. Sometimes this works—but mostly it fails, especially with men.

"Here in the East, a disciple literally follows Jesus' example. He will attempt to experience everything the Master experienced. You began this kind of discipleship here at Mount Athos."

The monk waited for me to jump in, but I simply stared at him. After a moment he asked, "Do you understand the lesson you learned?"

"No, I do not understand," I said, barely able to control my fury.

The monk took on a slightly condescending tone. "Then I must explain it to you. Think about your life back in America. You are powerful. You have money. A car. A home. Instant communication at your fingertips. A constitution that guarantees your rights and a military that protects your shores.

"When you decided to come here, you left all that behind. Your power was stripped away. Last night you had no protection. No rights. Your wealth was useless. You could communicate with no one. You were helpless. You had to spend the night in a stable, begging for food and transportation. You fled from men who might have been trying to kill you. Does this sound like anyone you know?"

My mind was blank, all thoughts blocked by a flood of

disappointment and rage. "Gerasimos, I'm tired of these riddles. Speak plainly for a change!"

The monk lowered his head and spoke softly. "He left his throne in heaven and became utterly powerless. He was born in a barn and slept in the hay. Men tried to kill him, but he fled to Egypt."

The truth bloomed in my soul like a morning flower. Powerlessness. Uncertainty. Deprivation. Danger. In the past twenty-four hours, Benson and I had gotten a small taste of what Jesus experienced in his first days on earth.

My heart was changed. A cool wave of gratitude washed over my white-hot anger. Gerasimos was right: because of what I'd just experienced, I felt that I *knew Jesus* in a new way. I had literally walked a path my Savior had. I was homeless. I slept in a stable. I ran for my life. In one day this Orthodox brother had taught me more about the Nativity than I had learned from a hundred Advent sermons.

I turned to Gerasimos. Once again contrition flowed. "I'm sorry, Teacher. There's no excuse for my outburst."

"This is true. Your temper will be your undoing," he said.

We were silent for a few moments. Finally, the monk spoke. "The events you experienced are only a small part of the first journey. Tomorrow I will reveal the entire path to you. I will speak plainly, as you requested."

"Tomorrow!" I cried. "Gerasimos, this is the fourth day. I'm already in trouble for overstaying my permit. If I miss my flight from Thessaloniki, how will I get back to the States?"

Gerasimos assaulted me again with those eyes. "My son, have you learned nothing? Be here at eight thirty tomorrow morning. Do not be late."

Chapter 8

TEMPEST

Remember those clouds I mentioned in the last chapter? They were the leading edge of a storm that struck just after midnight. I was fast asleep on the deck of the fisherman's boat when a stiff wind began blowing from the southeast. The vessel began rocking so hard I could barely keep myself from rolling into the gunwales. Then the heavens began to gush. I crawled over to the lockers where the tarps were kept and pulled one over my body. I huddled beneath it, fighting seasickness.

By 3:00 a.m. the storm intensified. Huge swells pitched the boat up and down. Rain seeped under the tarp as the vessel listed from side to side. I peeked from under my covering but couldn't see a shoreline. My world was a featureless, rolling, dripping maelstrom.

Then more fear: I thought I heard the anchor scraping along the bottom. If this was true, then the boat could be drifting out to the open sea—or toward the rocks. I crawled to the bow and donned a flotation vest, just in case. I was terrified, but I felt strangely alive at the same time. Eventually, the combination of blind fear and pounding waves brought a bout of nausea.

By four thirty, I was using what little strength I possessed to hang on to the captain's chair. I had never been so miserable, sick, and fatigued. My clothing was heavy and wet. There was no possibility of sleeping through this, and I was too weak to pray.

My weary mind recalled the New Testament accounts involving storms at sea. I thought, *How many more Bible stories will I have to relive on this trip?* At last I understood the disciples' ancient cry, "Lord, save us!"

By five, the squall abated somewhat. The rain dissolved into a mist, but the sea was still choppy. The sky had lightened a bit, and to my relief I could see the fisherman's hut off the starboard bow, right where it belonged. The anchor had held. A mixture of freshwater and saltwater dripped from the scuppers into the sea.

Suddenly the fisherman was at my side, speaking to me in Greek. Harsh morning light stabbed my eyes. *I must have fallen asleep sitting up.* I pried my fingers from the base of the captain's chair and crawled into his dinghy. I was weak and dehydrated from throwing up.

Back on terra firma, the fisherman knew just what to do. He took me inside and helped me strip off my wet clothing. Then he prepared a breakfast of peppermint tea, hot chicken broth, and pilot bread. Within half an hour I felt somewhat human again. The world had stopped rocking.

I checked my watch: 8:20. Gerasimos was expecting me in ten minutes. I found my bag and changed into some dry clothes. I washed my face and dragged myself up the narrow path, knees wobbling from fatigue.

I arrived at the monastery gate at 8:36. Gerasimos was not in the courtyard. *Please, God, tell me I didn't miss him.* Yet another monk was playing bouncer today. "Good morning," I croaked, not realizing my voice was shot from vomiting.

The monk said, "You will see Gerasimos?"

I nodded.

"Come," he said.

I had waited four days to walk through that doorway, and it was like traveling seven hundred years back in time. My eyes surveyed a world of hand-hewn stone arches, attached with ancient mortar and buttressed with blackened wood. The entire south wall of the monastery (the one facing the sea) was composed of individual cells, each with a small vent over a wooden door. Iron sconces sprang from the walls. To my left sat a Byzantine chapel, festooned with gold orbs and crosses. The ground level of the compound was a verdant lawn ringed with gardens, all meticulously tended.

The monk led me down a stone staircase to a plaster-covered building next to the chapel. Inside I found an exquisite library, its walls lined with books that looked to be centuries old. The smell of leather and parchment was intoxicating. The ceiling was adorned with icons and gold leaf.

A voice whispered from behind, "I told you not to be late."

I turned and saw Gerasimos. He was taken aback by my ragged appearance. "I'm sorry, Teacher," I rasped. "The sea was angry, but God was with me." My voice was so hoarse that whispering came naturally.

A tiny smile formed at the corners of the monk's lips. "Come, you have much to learn today." He dismissed the younger monk and led me on a brief tour of the library.

Gerasimos gestured toward the bookshelves. "Our collection is unrivaled on Athos. We have Christian-era documents dating back to the third century, and pre-Christian works from 700 BC." I was astounded. I had never seen such an assembly of ancient tomes. Despite the headache, my head spun madly to take it all in.

We came to a heavy wooden door, tucked into a corner of the building, almost invisible behind a bookshelf. "The answer you are looking for lies here," Gerasimos said. He pulled a gnarled key from his pocket and unlocked the bulky portal. I passed through cautiously as he secured the door behind us. We descended two sets of steep stairs, which was no simple feat in my weakened state. Gerasimos lit our way with a modern LED flashlight.

At last we arrived in a darkened basement. Gerasimos invited me to sit at a table while he unblocked a pair of stone ventilation outlets in the floor. Fresh air poured into the musty room. He then ignited a quartet of torches on the walls. The flickering torch light revealed deep shelves that held stacks of loose documents. Many appeared to be written on parchment or vellum. The monk disappeared behind one of the racks. Moments later, he returned to the table with a short stack of papers. To my surprise, these were not ancient parchments, but modern, typewritten pages.

"We can talk privately down here," he said. "I'm ready to explain the three journeys to you. I feel that the time is right for them to be shared with the world, and you are the man to do it," Gerasimos said.

There he goes with the three journeys again! I had no interest in his journeys. I wanted to know about the map. But out of respect for my teacher, I once again said nothing.

Brother Gerasimos sat down and began to tell his story. "About thirty years ago, when I was new to the monastery, I was assigned to catalog some documents in this room. I was on my knees sorting when I noticed that the lower panel of that bookshelf was loose." Gerasimos pointed a bony finger at one of the shelves. "I pulled on the panel and it came away easily. To my surprise, I found a very old parchment inside.

"The parchment was simply titled *The Three Journeys of Jesus*. It had been written by a Jewish convert to Christianity who called himself Justus of Sidon. We know nothing else about him. No other writings of his are known to exist.

"The document was unusual because it was written in three different tongues: Koine Greek, which is the language of the New Testament; Nabataean, an ancient Aramaic dialect; and a strange Hebrew variant I could not identify. Justus would switch freely between the languages, sometimes right in the middle of a sentence. I think this was his way of encoding the document so others could not read it."

Now Gerasimos had my undivided attention. He was telling me the other half of the tale that Isaac Kassif had shared with me in New Jersey. *Kassif must have been the man who translated the Hebrew and Nabataean sections*, I thought.

The monk continued his story: "For years I jealously guarded *The Three Journeys of Jesus*, even though I could only decipher the Greek parts. My ego was in charge—I preferred to be ignorant rather than share my discovery with anyone else.

"I eventually copied the Hebrew and Aramaic sections of the document character by character. This took years, because as a young Brother, I had very little free time, and my access to the lower reaches of the library was limited. I did not dare bring the document to my cell—for fear that it might be discovered.

"About five years ago, Father Spiro traveled from England to spend a few weeks at Pankronos. We happened to have lunch together one day, and he mentioned his expertise in Semitic languages. I took a chance and told him part of the truth. I brought him down here and presented him with my handmade copies of the Hebrew and Nabataean sections, hoping he could read them. I did not show him the original document.

"Spiro examined them, but the dialects were too obscure. He agreed to carry them to the Middle East and find expert translators. I swore him to secrecy. To my shame, I didn't tell Spiro about the Greek parts of the document because I didn't want him to unravel the whole mystery and take credit for the find.

"Three years later, Spiro returned to the monastery with the finished translations. But before he handed them to me, he asked me where I had found the documents. I felt the Spirit of Jesus urging me to reveal everything.

"Spiro was astonished by what I told him, and he agreed to help me combine the translations right away. He went to the abbot and got special permission for the two of us to travel to a secluded area of Athos for seven days of prayer and fasting. But we did not fast. Instead, Spiro and I spent the week piecing the fragments into one coherent work. For a man in his nineties, he brought amazing zest to this labor."

Gerasimos brushed his hand across the document. "This is our final product—a modern Greek translation of *The Three Journeys of Jesus*. You are looking at the only copy." Gerasimos gently flipped through the pages. They had been typed on an old-fashioned, Greek-language manual typewriter. I couldn't read a word, but even so I knew I was looking at something priceless.

"Teacher," I said, "I have something important to tell you. I met the man who translated the Hebrew and Nabataean sections of this document. His name is Isaac Kassif, and he's the reason I'm here."

Gerasimos's eyes flashed. "What do you know of this man?"

I told him the entire story: from the moment Benson gave me Kassif's e-mail address, to my trip to New York, to the mysterious envelope shoved under my hotel room door. I told him that Kassif had asked me to help him find the rest of the manuscript—and that Kassif was searching for a map.

Gerasimos stroked his beard. He looked troubled. "Kassif sent you here?"

"He did. He paid all my expenses."

"And he believes there is a map? Drawn by one of the twelve apostles?"

"Yes," I said. "Isn't there one?"

The monk did not answer. I could almost hear his synapses firing. "This Kassif should not have known my identity. I did not know his until you revealed it this very moment. Spiro kept our names confidential. Of that I am sure."

Then a thought occurred to me. "Gerasimos, didn't Kassif tell you we were coming?"

"No. As I told you, I had never heard of him. Your arrival at the monastery came as a complete surprise. I knew of Benson, and his relationship with Spiro. Therefore, I assumed that Spiro had sent you on a spiritual pilgrimage, in order to learn the three journeys. When I found out you were a well-known author, I spent the night in prayer, asking Jesus if you were his chosen vessel to communicate the three journeys to the wider world. For this reason I have been testing you."

Now it was all coming clear to me. The long waits at the monastery. Gerasimos's sharp rebuke and obscure lessons. The monk thought we were pilgrims and had been treating us as disciples in search of revelation.

I asked, "Teacher, you are aware that Father Spiro is dead?"

Gerasimos looked surprised. "No, I was unaware. How did it happen?"

"He died the day I was to visit him at the vicarage. Benson thinks someone may have taken his life."

The two of us sat in the basement, staring at the table. The only sound was the flickering of torches. Finally, Gerasimos spoke: "Do you see what has happened? Kassif is searching for a map, hand-drawn by one of the twelve apostles. Such a map would be worth millions to a wealthy private collector. If Kassif is truly a scholar and man of peace, then we have nothing to fear. But if he is a treasure hunter, he will stop at nothing to acquire this map."

The monk cocked his head. "Kassif probably sent a man to go through Spiro's papers. That is how he discovered my name." Gerasimos looked up and stared into my eyes. "David, Kassif may be using you to acquire the knowledge he seeks. If so, he will attempt to extract that knowledge as soon as you leave the safety of these walls."

Fear impaled my heart. Mentally, I was back on the boat, fighting the waves. The stone floor began rocking back and forth. The torches on the walls were spinning. Before I could recover, Gerasimos piled on more bad news. "At a minimum, you must change your travel plans back to the United States. You might also take steps to protect your loved ones at home. Get them to a safe place. Immediately."

For the first time in my life, I was so frightened I could not think. A punishing combination of fear, exhaustion, de-hydration, and hunger had dropped me into neutral. I stared at the floor, worrying about my family in Alaska. *What a fool I've been. Like a bored teenager, I took this adventure on a lark.*

My carelessness may have put my loved ones at risk! Are they all right? I had no way of knowing. I felt utterly powerless—weaker than the night I'd spent in the barn or at the mercy of the sea. Emotionally, I was descending into the belly of the whale, and I could see no way out.

The monk grabbed me by the shoulders and looked me in the eyes. The righteous fire was gone, replaced with a deep sorrow. "David, hear my confession. My lust for recognition and fame has placed you in jeopardy. I wanted to be the discoverer of a great truth, but by hiding God's light under a basket, I've allowed the forces of darkness to gather. Will you forgive me?"

I stared into his weathered face. Gerasimos's humble words broke my panic. A voice in my heart said, *Trust this man. He can help you.* An irrational peace washed over my soul. Words came to my lips that were not my own. "Yes, Gerasimos, I forgive you. Now, what should we do?"

"Jesus has already revealed the answer," he said. "He told the apostles, 'The truth will set you free.' We must speak the truth—and do so as quickly as possible."

"What do you mean?" I asked.

"Any tomb raider knows there is money to be made by keeping an ancient artifact hidden. But once the discovery is announced, Kassif cannot profit. The game is over, and we are safe."

I'm not usually attuned to the spiritual world, but for a brief moment I thought I could hear the distant sound of clashing swords. A battle was raging over the document that rested on the table in front of me. Or was the battle for my soul? Gerasimos had tested my faith, but his lessons were merely the undercard. Now came the main event. I had stepped out of the boat and trusted the Lord to a point, but with the waves crashing about me, fear had taken the upper hand. That moment I realized how truly weak my faith was.

Once again, Gerasimos seemed to understand. He placed a hand on my shoulder and said, "Don't be afraid. God is with us. Keep in mind that none of this may be true. Kassif might just be a curious scholar. If so, then there is no danger."

Right. A curious scholar who passes out fifteen-thousand-dollar plane tickets to strangers. There was little doubt Isaac Kassif was using me to get to the map—and that I had fallen into his trap. I spoke forcefully to Gerasimos. "All right. If the truth sets us free, then it's time for you to tell me the truth. Everything. And speak plainly. Let's start with the map."

———— *Chapter 9* ————

REVELATION

Gerasimos pulled a blank sheet of paper from the bottom of the stack. "Tell me again what Kassif said about the map. Something about Joshua and Levi?"

"He said that Joshua had given the map to Levi, and Levi had hidden it with his scroll. Kassif was puzzled by this, until I told him that Joshua can be translated *Yeshua*, or Jesus, and that Levi is another name for Matthew."

"Very good. You solved that part of the riddle. But Kassif made one critical translation error. The Hebrew word for *with* can sometimes be translated *in*. Justus of Sidon was actually saying that Jesus gave the map to Matthew and that he hid it *in* his scroll. The map is not a separate document."

"What do you mean?"

"There is no map, drawn on paper by an apostle. The artifact Kassif seeks does not exist. However, there is a map, written in code, hidden in the gospel of Matthew. Justus of Sidon discovered the code, which enabled him to draw the map."

Now I was really confused. *A secret map? Encoded in the gospel of Matthew?* Once again I was reminded of *The Da Vinci Code*. The very idea was shocking to my evangelical sensibilities. I stared at the teacher. "Are you suggesting that Matthew took liberties with the Word of God?"

"You do not understand Jewish custom," Gerasimos said. "It was common practice for Hebrew writers to embed patterns, numbers, and codes into their sacred writings. These codes revealed important information about the text—and the rabbi who wrote it. Jewish disciples were taught to decipher these codes in order to gain a deeper understanding of the rabbi himself."

I was skeptical. "Do all the Gospels contain codes?" I asked.

"I don't think so. According to Justus, only Matthew did this. I've studied all four gospels, and I agree: Matthew is the only gospel that contains a code like this one."

"Why only Matthew?"

"Because Matthew is the most Jewish of the four gospels. Matthew had an agenda: he was clearly trying to convince his fellow Hebrews that Jesus is Messiah. For example, Matthew started his account with a genealogy and included more references to the Old Testament than any of the other gospel writers. Since Matthew was writing to Jews, it would be perfectly natural for him to follow Hebraic custom and put codes and patterns into his account."

I was beginning to believe. "Okay, so where is this code? How can I find it?"

Gerasimos pulled a ballpoint pen from inside his cassock. "I will show you how to find it in a moment. But first I will draw the map for you." The monk quickly sketched the shape of a mountain. "The three journeys can easily be translated into a map. In fact, Justus drew a sketch like this in his original manuscript. It mystified me for years because the key was written in Nabataean.

"This mountain represents a man's identity—his nature, or his ego. Inside every man's heart is the desire to reach the summit: to become a great man. Yet very few men even set foot on this mountain—much less get to the top."

Gerasimos drew the female symbol ♀ on the left side of the map and the male symbol ♂ on the right.

He continued, "As a man progresses through life, he must develop and balance the two sides of his nature: the soft, accepting, feminine side and the hard, demanding, masculine side. The left side of the map represents the feminine traits as defined by classical Greek philosophers: contemplation, relationships, receptivity, and emotion, to name a few. Meanwhile, the right side of the map represents traditional masculine traits: action, achievement, hierarchy, and power. A truly great man must conquer both sides of the mountain if he is to reach the pinnacle."

I nodded but said nothing.

Gerasimos began drawing at the lower left corner of the paper. "Look at the bottom of the map. A man starts his natural life journey here—on the feminine side. Every man spends the first nine months of life inside the body of a woman. At birth the boy breaks free from the woman and begins a lifelong journey to identify himself as a man. This journey starts slowly. Little boys are not much concerned with their gender, but young men become obsessed with manliness, pushing themselves to extreme displays

of daring and courage. This pursuit is universal, observed among men in every culture on the globe."

The monk drew a series of small hills at the base of the mountain's right flank. "So for the first twenty years or so, most men move as far as they can away from femininity, and they end up here.

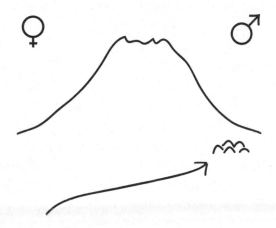

"These foothills represent a stunted manhood—violent, self-centered, power hungry, and unmerciful. You Americans have a good name for these foothills: *macho*. Some men never progress beyond macho—they remain obsessed with manliness their entire lives. They stand on these little hills, beat their chests, and scream to the world, 'Look at me! I am a man!'

"But some men wake up and realize that they are not climbing the mountain of manhood at all. These men hear the call of Christ and want to follow him. Now they have a frightening decision to make." Gerasimos drew a line from the foothills to the left side of the map.

"Any mountaineer knows you cannot climb a mountain by going straight up. And so it is with the three journeys. A man who would follow the path of Jesus must first go back

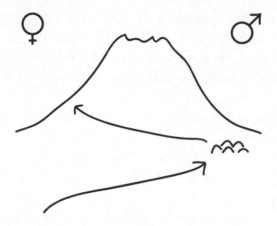

in the feminine direction he has been fleeing his entire life. Justus called this *the journey of submission*."

The teacher paused to let the term sink in. Then he continued, "The men who walk the first journey embrace the humility of our Lord. A first-journey Christian must reject his own strength, power, and intelligence and take up weakness, dependence, and reliance on Jesus. He must learn to love God and to be loved by God. Submission is the foundation of a successful walk with Christ.

"No other religion demands that men begin their spiritual journey by moving so deliberately toward a feminine set of values and behaviors. For this reason, many men reject Christianity. Other men accept the teachings of Christ, but they fail to become men of faith because it requires them to backtrack, psychologically speaking. It's easier for men to lie to themselves and pretend that the foothills *are* the pinnacle of manhood."

Fascinating. I thought about my teen years and my own struggle to prove my manliness. It wasn't a conscious thing, but my need to be manly was the driving force behind many of my actions and decisions. Then I recalled the months following my conversion—how I gave up stereotypical macho behaviors and embraced attitudes my friends would consider girlish, including weakness, gentleness, and self-control. Psychologically, my early faith walk had indeed moved me away from classic manliness, though I didn't realize it at the time.

Before I could fully grasp the implications of the first journey, Gerasimos continued the lesson: "Once a man learns to submit, he must not stop there. The disciple begins a second journey in the opposite direction. Justus called this *the journey of strength*. Having submitted himself to Christ, the man accepts the power God gives him and does not run from it. He resumes his pursuit of manliness, but at a higher level. This second journey is a lifelong process of discerning, executing, and completing the mission to which God has called the man.

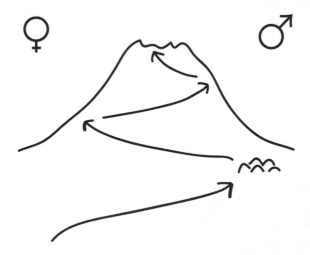

"There is a third journey, which Justus called *the journey of sacrifice*. It is a second, deeper submission than the first. Sacrifice is a final, voluntary relinquishing of strength and power. It is the closing act of life, and it takes a man in the feminine direction once more—toward weakness, vulnerability, and a complete love for Christ. The pilgrim lays down his life for the next generation to carry the mission forward. As you can imagine, this is the most difficult journey. Very few even attempt this path. Fewer still reach the summit. No, most men who begin the three journeys get lost somewhere on the mountain."

"Lost? How?" I asked.

Gerasimos pointed to the left flank of the mountain. "Many men stop here, on the feminine side. They walk in submission their entire lives but never progress to strength. Nowhere is this more apparent than here in the monastery. Monastic tradition emphasizes the first and last journeys while ignoring the middle one. Monks are very good at submission, and we are experts at sacrifice. But when it comes to strength, we're like cannonballs neatly stacked, ready for battle, but never fired."

I spoke up. "We have the same problem in the local church. Congregations are full of nice guys who sit in the pews year after year but who never fully engage."

Gerasimos nodded. "Then we have other men who omit the first journey and proceed right to the second. They try to go straight up the mountain." The monk drew a line from the foothills up the right flank of the mountain. "They attempt to serve God from their own strength. These men bring their sin, ambition, and lust for power into the church. They think they are serving God, but they are not true followers of Jesus because their walk is not rooted in humility. Such men do more harm than good."

Gerasimos stood and walked over to the bookshelf. He retrieved a musty English-language New International Version Bible that looked to be from the 1970s. "I want to show you Matthew's code. Are you ready to see it?"

I was still absorbed in the map. The monk placed the Bible on the table and flipped through its worn pages. "First, you must see the place where Jesus speaks of the map. It's in Matthew 7, verses 13 and 14. Read it to me." Gerasimos pushed the open Bible across the table.

> "Enter through the narrow gate. For wide is the gate and broad is the road that leads to destruction, and many enter through it. But small is the gate and narrow the road that leads to life, and only a few find it."

The teacher tapped on the verse. "In a brilliant piece of reasoning, Justus realized this passage was a clue. Since Jesus is speaking of a road, he thought, *Perhaps there is a map*. Justus began looking, and it wasn't long before he found and deciphered the code and re-created the map."

I was unconvinced. "Gerasimos, I've always taken this passage as a metaphor for heaven and hell. How did Justus realize it pointed to a code?"

"These two verses are somewhat out of place in the Sermon on the Mount.[1] They directly follow a verse that sounds like the sermon's conclusion.[2] And Matthew is the only gospel writer who includes the passage. In America, you would say that these verses stick out like a sore finger."

"Sore thumb," I said.

Gerasimos ignored my correction. "How many times have you read from the gospel of Matthew?" he asked.

I thought about it. "Hundreds. Maybe a thousand, if you count small groups and readings in church."

Gerasimos gestured at the Bible. "Then you've looked at the code a thousand times, but you've never seen it." He thumbed through the pages until he arrived at the first chapter of Matthew. "Did you ever notice that sometimes Jesus was meek and compassionate, but other times he seemed

powerful and somewhat arrogant? It's almost as if there are two Christs in the Bible, no?"

"Yes, I've seen that. Sometimes he's like a lion, and other times he's like a lamb," I said.

"Exactly," the teacher exclaimed. "Mark, Luke, and John mix the lion and lamb passages together freely. You never know from verse to verse which Christ you'll find. But Matthew reveals the two sides of Christ's personality in a very deliberate order."

Gerasimos began flipping through the first chapters of Matthew. "In Matthew chapters 1 through 7, Jesus is almost completely lamb. He's born as a helpless babe, in utter poverty. He submits to baptism, even though he has no sins to wash away. He receives the love of his Father. He weakens himself through fasting. He gives himself over to temptation. Then he preaches the Sermon on the Mount, whose great themes are 'Blessed are the meek' and 'Turn the other cheek.'"

The monk turned to Matthew 8, eyes aflame. "But when Jesus comes down that mountain, he transforms into a lion. He begins his famous battles with the Pharisees. He fights with demons, commands the forces of nature, and feeds the multitudes. He fires sharp rebukes at both friend and foe. He curses unrepentant cities and warns of coming destruction. From chapter 8 through chapter 25, he is the Lion of Judah.

"Then, suddenly, in chapter 26, Jesus becomes a lamb again. He refuses to defend himself when he's falsely arrested and accused. He rebukes one of his men for using a sword. He allows himself to be tortured, mocked, and killed, even though it is within his power to stop it. He is the sacrificial lamb of God."

Matthew 1–7	Matthew 8–25	Matthew 26–28
Submission	Strength	Sacrifice
♀	♂	♀

The teacher's voice rose. "Do you see it now? The first seven chapters of Matthew represent the journey of submission. The following eighteen chapters portray the journey of strength. The final three chapters demonstrate the journey of sacrifice. These are the paths our Savior walked. Therefore, if we truly desire to follow Jesus, we must walk these three paths as well."

Gerasimos paused so I could absorb all that he was saying. He was right: I'd looked at Matthew's gospel hundreds of times but had never seen the pattern. However, Justus of Sidon had taken the high view. He saw the broad strokes in Matthew's account. He recognized them for what they are: a code that reveals the one and only path that makes a man a complete disciple.

"Wait a minute," I said. "You're saying that Matthew altered the order of events in Jesus' life to create this code?"

Gerasimos was ready. "There is wide consensus among Bible scholars that the gospel of Matthew is not a chronological, event-by-event telling of the life of Jesus—nor was it intended to be. As I said, this account was written to a Jewish audience, and in that culture, context is more important than chronology. It's clear that Matthew was trying to show future disciples *how* to follow Jesus by arranging his telling this way. The order of events is a simple Hebraic code."

The monk closed the Bible and picked up his hand-sketched map. "Matthew's code reveals two important truths: First, disciples of Jesus must walk three journeys—submission,

then strength, then sacrifice. And second, these journeys must be taken in the proper order. Any deviation from this path leads to destruction."

"What do you mean?" I asked.

"Justus observed that many of the Bible's greatest heroes also walked the three journeys. Those who completed the journeys in the right order became great and succeeded in their mission. Moses, for example. But those who deviated from the pattern ended up in trouble. King David comes to mind."

"King David?" I asked. "Wasn't he a man after God's heart?"

"David completely embraced submission, and he certainly walked in strength. But he failed the journey of sacrifice. His negligence brought civil war into his house and untold suffering to Israel."

I nodded. This was beginning to make more sense.

"David, you claim to be a disciple, yet you are not a disciple in the classic Jewish sense. In ancient times, to be a disciple meant that you would imitate your rabbi in every way. For example, if your rabbi was left-handed, then you became left-handed. If your rabbi took a pilgrimage to Jacob's tomb at age twenty-five, then you would be expected to make the same journey when you achieved that age. If your rabbi wore thirty-six tassels on his robe, then you would too. In other words, you were obliged not only to follow the teachings of your rabbi, but also to pattern your life after his. Do you see what I am saying?"

"Yes, I think so."

"In a spiritual sense, a disciple dies to himself, and his rabbi lives through him. Even after a rabbi passes on, his disciples would be like clones of the rabbi, doing things exactly as he would, extending the rabbi's life and influence down through the generations."

I spoke up. "So when the apostle Paul wrote, 'It is no longer I who live, but Christ who lives in me,' he was thinking like a Hebrew disciple."

"Yes. In Jewish culture, a disciple is more than a student; he is an exact copy of his rabbi. This is why Paul admonished Christians to be imitators of him, even as he imitated Christ. But how are we to imitate our rabbi if we do not know his life pattern? We need more than his teachings; we need insight into the way he lived and how he became the man he was. That is what the map tells us—Jesus became great first through submission, then through strength, and finally through sacrifice. As his followers, we must walk these three paths in the same sequence he did."

I marveled at the simplicity and brilliance of Justus's ancient thesis. "Now that I see the three journeys, they seem so obvious. How were they lost?"

"Matthew made a strategic error—he assumed the church was going to remain a Jewish institution, led by rabbis who would see the code clearly. But by the year 150, the church was almost completely Gentile. Jewish ways of thinking were replaced by Greco-Roman ones. Eventually, even Jewish Christians lost their ability to read the code. So the map has been sitting there, hidden in plain view for centuries, printed in every copy of the New Testament."

I picked up the mountain sketch and marveled. "Teacher, a finding of this importance could change the church. It will certainly change how men approach discipleship."

"This has been my constant prayer," he said. "The reason the men in your churches are so impotent is because they have no sense of progress. They practice their religion, but they do not feel that it is leading them toward something greater. When men are not advancing up a path, they disengage. Eventually, they fall away."

I began to see great power in this simple diagram. It could bring some order to the random, chaotic way our churches approach disciple making. It could give men the goal they secretly crave. And it could provide men a framework in which to explore the feminine virtues. I was hungry to know more. "Gerasimos, the lessons you taught us—will you interpret them for me?"

"You interpret them!" The monk stood and began pacing. "Your first lesson came even before we began driving." He pointed a finger up the stairs. "When you two arrived at the monastery, I made you wait, in order to test your resolve. So you waited and waited. Finally, I came to you in humility, posing as a gardener, but you did not recognize me. You rejected me. When I came the second time, there was no doubt as to my identity. You treated me with the proper respect. Now, interpret the lesson."

I shook my head. "I'm sorry, Teacher. I don't understand. What does it mean?"

"Are you completely blind? The Jews waited hundreds of years for the Messiah. He finally came, but as a humble servant, so they did not recognize him. They expected a king but got a carpenter. They rejected him. However, when Messiah appears a second time, every knee will bow. There will be no doubt as to his identity."

I was silent. My temples were throbbing—whether with enlightenment or dehydration, I wasn't sure.

"Now, as to your formal lessons: How about the compass needle? What did that lesson mean?"

I thought for a moment. "We started by driving away

from the mountain. You said that the first journey of Jesus takes a man away from the direction he wants to go—toward feminine virtues. The second journey takes him the way he wants to go—back to the masculine. The third journey takes him back again—to the feminine."

"You are correct. A road is an odd thing, often taking you away from your destination in order to take you toward it. In the same way, the journeys of Jesus sometimes lead you away from manliness in order to make you a complete man."

Gerasimos kept teaching. "David, what about the second lesson? The men working with horses?"

I knew the answer right away. "There are three steps to a horse's development: Step one is breaking the horse, or teaching it submission. Step two is working the horse, or using its strength. Step three is going to stud, or sacrificing its genetic material for the next generation of horses."

"Good. Now what about the lesson of the abandoned building?"

This one stumped me, so Gerasimos explained, "When erecting a building, you lay the foundation first, then the structure, and finally the roof. Submission is like the foundation: it underlies everything. A firm foundation will keep the building standing through the most violent storm. Strength is like the building itself. It's the part you live in, and the one visitors notice when they enter. Sacrifice is like the roof, protecting the people and goods therein. Do you understand?"

"Yes, Teacher," I said.

"Now, do you remember the fourth lesson? I asked you to name all the cities you stopped in, from New York to tiny Daphne."

"Yes, that lesson is very confusing," I said.

"No, it's very simple. As you move up the mountain, fewer

and fewer men will join you. A thousand eager pilgrims begin the journey of submission, but only one hundred complete it. Of these just ten will complete the journey of strength. And only one will complete the journey of sacrifice."

I gestured toward the racks of ancient parchments. "Gerasimos, I need to be writing this down."

The teacher shook his head. "You will not forget these parables, because you personally experienced them. This is how men learn. Why do you think there are so many parables in the Bible? Jesus preached many public sermons, but just one survives. However, many of his parables live to this day because men just like you remembered them."

I sighed. "I know better than to ask this, but I'm having trouble concentrating because I'm hungry. I was seasick in the storm last night, and this morning all I had was broth and a cracker. I'm feeling a bit nauseous again. Do you have anything to eat?"

A faint smile tugged at the monk's lips. "I can hardly believe it. The secrets of heaven are being revealed, and all you can think of is your stomach." Gerasimos returned the documents to their hiding place, closed the floor vents, and doused the torches. He led me up the stairs, teaching as we went. "The lesson of the chestnut tree—have you figured it out?"

"That one is also hard," I said.

Gerasimos stopped on the first landing. "The journey of submission is like a seed. In a spiritual sense, the disciple falls into the ground and dies—to self, to ambition, to worldly pleasure. This act of submission forms the foundation of the tree, which emerges from the ground in a journey of strength, growing larger and larger, beyond anyone's dreams. The tree's final disposition is sacrifice. Maybe it falls to the ground and rots. It might be consumed in a fire. Or it could be used for timber, or firewood, or furniture. It might become a book or a chair or a violin. Hear me: the final disposition of the tree depends on the qualities it acquires during journeys one and two."

I was speechless, astonished at the monk's depth and insight. Before I could fully grasp his latest tutorial, he was moving up the stairs, teaching over his shoulder. "David, there was one more lesson—the most important of all. Do you recall it?"

I shook my throbbing head.

"Remember when we ran out of fuel? I sent you and Benson to get some from the farmer. Tell me, which way were you walking: toward the monastery or away from it?"

"Away," I said.

"That walk represented the journey of submission. You were moving away from your goal. You were powerless. You had no fuel. You did not speak the language. At the farmhouse you acquired some fuel. Then you began walking back toward your goal, with power in your hands. This second walk represented the journey of strength. You were filled with hope. You had what you had come for. But you were unable to find me. So you went back in the direction you did not want to go— away from the monastery. Once again you were powerless. Stalked by danger. Your third walk represented sacrifice."

"Incredible," I said. "And I suppose you ordered that storm last night to teach me another lesson?"

"No, that squall was a gift from God. So was Benson's incarceration. The apostles got seasick and spent many nights in jail. Now you have tasted those as well."

Chapter 10

THE AWAKENING

Gerasimos led me out of the library into a sunlit garden. The sky was back to its cloudless norm. We crossed a court-yard and entered the back door of a large kitchen. A short, friendly monk served me a bowl of hearty soup and a slab of spent grain bread.

The teacher and I stepped back outdoors and sat on a bench. As I lapped up my soup, a fusillade of questions came to my lips: "How does a man know what journey he is on? How do you know when you've completed one journey and you're ready for the next? Is it possible to exercise strength while still working on submission?"

"You will spend the rest of your life pondering these mysteries," he said. "But think again of the horse. There comes a day when he is 'submitted' enough to begin work. The cowboy knows when his mount is ready. The beast isn't aware that anything has changed, other than his daily routine. And so it is with the journeys. When you have given enough of your strength over to God in submission, he begins giving his strength back to you. Your job is to receive it."

The monk continued, "Even a good horse might

occasionally forget its early training and throw a rider. The journeys are somewhat elastic in this way. You will have setbacks. The important thing is to move forward in your journeys. You never fully complete a journey, but as you progress through your spiritual life, the emphasis changes. And the more quickly you learn submission, the sooner God can use you for greater things."

I had finished my soup and was gnawing on a crust of bread, feeling much better with something in my stomach. Gerasimos took my empty bowl and said, "You must rest. I will present our situation to God, and then I will hear his plan. Come." He led me over worn stone pavements and up a set of narrow stairs. I longed to drink in the beauty of this place, but Gerasimos's brisk pace made that impossible.

The monk opened a small cell on the second level. "This is where guests stay," he said. The stone walls were unadorned, except for a single icon depicting the monastery's patron saint. The floors were composed of rough wooden timbers. An arched window frame provided a breathtaking view of the Aegean, although the aperture contained no glass—only wooden shutters. On the right sat a chair and a table holding a plain white porcelain washbasin and a fresh hand towel. There was no plumbing, only a stoneware pitcher, a mug, and a covered chamber pot. To the left I saw a cot with a cushion, blanket, and pillows.

A bed! It had been almost a week since I'd slept in anything resembling one. I lay down and felt secure inside the monastery's thick walls. I took a moment to pray for my family's safety, but fatigue cut my petitions short. I fell into a deep sleep, soothed by the sea breeze and the sound of crashing waves a hundred meters below my window.

In case you were wondering, a monastery is a great place

to take a nap. It's absolutely quiet all day. I slept almost six hours, hardly moving a muscle. When I finally awoke, sunlight was dancing off the face of the sea, projecting waves of light on the ceiling of my cell. I stared at the light show for a couple of minutes, stretched my body, and turned to my left.

My heart stopped. Sitting in my room was one of the Russians. It was Nikolai—or was it Pavel? I couldn't speak.

"Hello, Sir," said the monk. "Did you sleep well?"

"Where is Gerasimos?" I asked.

"He is ready to go. I was just preparing to waken you."

In my grogginess I couldn't remember if this man was friend or foe. He stood and went to the door, tapping on it lightly. The other Russian stepped into the room. He nodded his head to acknowledge me and began speaking to his compatriot. I could not understand their words.

After a minute, the taller of the two spoke to me. "Mr. Murrow, Gerasimos has asked us to take you to Stravnokita. You will be safer there."

"I feel safe here," I said. I did not trust these men.

The monks looked at each other, as if to say, *Haven't we had this conversation before?* They exchanged a few more words in Russian. "Mr. Murrow, please, time is short. We must be back before dark."

"I want to see Gerasimos," I said defiantly.

"Of course. Come with us."

We stepped out of the cell into a deserted courtyard. There was not a monk to be seen. Either they were at afternoon prayers (likely), or the Russians had killed them all and thrown their bodies into the sea (very unlikely). The men led me through the courtyard, up the stairs, and toward the exit door. I stopped. "I'm not going any farther," I said.

"We are taking you to Gerasimos," said the tall one. "He is already in the car."

Already in the car? I imagined the teacher's body stuffed into the trunk. Then my mind cleared enough to recall the teacher's words from yesterday: *"I sent Pavel and Nikolai as another test—to trust or not to trust."* As suspicious as these two characters were, they had helped Gerasimos before. But what if they were double agents who had befriended Gerasimos to get to the map? They and their Mercedes could be in the employ of Isaac Kassif. I began walking again, considering my next move with each step.

We exited the monastery through the courtyard. I made a point to say good-bye to the monk so he could have a good look at our faces. The doorman smiled as we left the compound. Ahead I could see the black Mercedes sedan parked under the monastery arch. The sun was low at our backs. I could not tell if the car held a passenger.

I stopped about one hundred meters from the car. "Hold on. My bag is down at the fisherman's house. I need to go down and get it."

The short Russian spoke. "Your bag is already in the back. It has an interesting smell," he said with a slight grimace.

We began walking again. I felt like a man headed for a firing squad. In another fifty meters I would know my fate. "Wait!" I said. "Please, stay here. I want to speak to Gerasimos. Alone."

The tall monk smiled. "Of course. But please, be quick," he said, pointing at the reddening sun.

I power-walked toward the sedan, glancing behind me. The monks were slowly following. I reached for the passenger door and flung it open. Sitting in the backseat was Gerasimos, unconscious. "Teacher!" I cried.

The monk opened his eyes. Apparently, he had been deep in meditation. "David, did you sleep well?"

"Yes, Teacher. Are you all right?"

Gerasimos nodded. "I am fine. Nikolai and Pavel are taking us to their monastery, Stravnokita. I fear we are not safe here."

I looked at the car's rich leather interior. "Can we trust these men?"

"Yes, yes! Don't be fooled; they have a generous patron."

Within a minute the four of us were seated in the Mercedes. Nikolai took the wheel and gunned the engine. As we sped down the narrow road, Gerasimos explained that Mount Athos is home to twenty monasteries: seventeen Greek, one Serbian, one Bulgarian, and one Russian. Stravnokita enjoys the best of everything, thanks to the patronage of a wealthy Russian oil tycoon. Their abbot has a saying: "I took a vow of poverty. The monastery took no such vow."

It took the Mercedes less than thirty minutes to arrive at Stravnokita. This cloister was on the north side of the peninsula, built on flat lowland near the sea. It looked just as ancient as Pankronos, but even in the gathering dusk I noticed a satellite dish atop one of the buildings. As we got out of the car, I heard the muted hum of a diesel generator from somewhere in the compound.

After a simple meal of boiled meat, cabbage, and potatoes, an English-speaking monk named Mikhail led me up a set of ancient stairs, where he unlocked a metal door. Inside was a modern communications room. It featured a trio of Internet-enabled computers and several telephones. "We have satellite communication links. Here are the instructions to call the United States." Mikhail handed me a tattered card written in

English, French, and Italian. He stepped back and said, "You may wish to know that a friend of the monastery has opened an investigation into Isaac Kassif." He bowed and closed the door behind me.

I called my wife in Alaska. She was preparing breakfast for the kids.

There is no worse duty for a husband than to tell his wife that she and her children may be in danger—and that hubby is to blame. She cried twice, but to her credit she mostly held her composure. I told her to take the kids and fly out to a remote lodge in the Wrangell Mountains operated by a couple in our church. We thought up a cover story: she and the kids were joining me in Greece for an extended holiday. She was to misinform her parents and a few key friends and then vanish that afternoon. I promised to contact her when the coast was clear. School didn't start for another month; hopefully we'd have a resolution before then.

The next morning, Gerasimos began translating *The Three Journeys of Jesus* from Greek into English. Meanwhile, I started on the book you hold in your hands. We put in twelve-hour days, under the protection and patronage of the Russian abbot.

On September 12, sixty days after I arrived in Greece, Gerasimos and I held a press conference in Athens to announce the discovery of *The Three Journeys of Jesus*. It made worldwide news. We made sure that reporters understood that the map was a metaphorical one, not an actual parchment. I also mentioned that my new book would be released in the United States under the title *The Map: The Way of All Great Men*.

I am told that worldwide Bible sales spiked on the announcement, and church attendance even got a little bump.

I waited until that evening to call my wife. I had not spoken to her in seven weeks. By then it was morning in the Wrangell Mountains. It took some effort to get through on the satellite phone, and with calls running five dollars a minute, we didn't have much time to talk. I only got a few words out when she burst into tears. A certified blubbering mess. Then I fell apart. It was one of the most expensive (and satisfying) cries we've ever shared.

Two days later, I met her and the kids at Anchorage International Airport. It was a grand reunion with smiles all around, until the little ones realized that their extended summer vacation had ended and they would have to go to school the next day.

Benson and I spent a lot of time in front of the cameras over the next month or so. But after a while the media frenzy died, and the two of us went back to normalcy. We talk regularly by e-mail, and I'm trying to get him over to Alaska for a visit next summer, to show him what *real* fishing is about.

And Isaac Kassif? I never heard from him again. Maybe our Russian friends took care of him. Only God knows.

PART TWO

The Three Journeys

Chapter 11

DISCOVERING THE MAP

I have a confession to make.

None of the events in the past ten chapters actually happened. Benson, Spiro, Kassif, Justus of Sidon, and Gerasimos—I made them all up.[1] Secret maps, murders, Mercedes—I *wish* my life were that adventurous.

But the map is real. Here's how I actually discovered it. One morning I was sitting in my favorite chair, wearing my pajamas, reading from the Bible. I was curious: *How was Jesus able to balance the masculine and feminine sides of his personality?*

As I opened the gospel of Matthew, I heard a voice in my head say, *Speed-read.*

So I skimmed. I looked at the forest instead of the trees. And suddenly, there it was—a map to manhood—written in a simple Hebraic code. I deciphered the code and turned it into an actual map in a matter of minutes.

And that's how I discovered the map. Sitting in a chair, reading a Bible, wearing my jammies. Thrilling, huh? I think you can see why I decided to spice up the story just a bit.

Now, why a map?

I don't know about you, but I have always loved maps. I think most men do. It has to do with the male brain's visual/spatial abilities. I would much rather navigate from a map than from verbal directions like these:

> Okay, go for a little bit, then turn by the big green flowerpot, then follow the fence for a little while until it curves, and there will be this big oak tree, but don't turn there . . . Keep going until you see the pink mailbox surrounded by flowering hydrangeas, then make a left and then a quick right. Then go two or three streets past the windmill . . .

Now, think about how we train men to follow Jesus. Do we give them a map to follow? No, men come to church and get verbal directions! Sermons, Bible studies, classes, seminars, books—it's a snowstorm of words. Even the Bible—that wonderful, divinely inspired book—is a collection of verbal directions.

No wonder so many men are meandering, even the ones who want to follow Christ. I've attended church for more than thirty years, and not once have I seen a map of the path I'm supposed to be walking. Week after week I sit in church and get verbal directions.

Please don't misunderstand me. I'm not saying that Scripture is inadequate or that men are ignorant Neanderthals who can't learn from books or sermons. But golly gee willikers, wouldn't it be easier on men if they had a map that *showed* them the route to a fulfilling life? A chart to help them navigate the Venus/Mars thing? Think that might be a game changer?

That's why I'm so excited about finding Matthew's map.

At last, men have a simple, ink-on-paper chart of the path that leads to life (Matthew 7:13–14).

––––––––––––

Want to see Matthew's code for yourself? Just do what I did. Grab a New Testament and skim the gospel of Matthew. Observe the broad contours of Jesus' life and teaching. Note when he's a lion and when he's a lamb (in both word and deed).

This pattern will emerge:

- Matthew 1–7: Jesus is *mostly* humble, meek, and submissive. His life and teachings reflect a classic feminine pattern.
- Matthew 8–25: Jesus is *mostly* powerful, bold, and outspoken. His life and teachings reflect a classic masculine pattern.
- Matthew 26–28: Jesus is *mostly* meek, passive, and sacrificial. His life once again reflects a classic feminine pattern.

Before we go any further, let's not run aground on the words *masculine* and *feminine*. I'm not saying that strength is manly and submission is womanly. I'm simply pointing out that, throughout the literature of a thousand cultures, attributes such as strength, aggression, goal orientation, competitiveness, and conflict are most often identified as male. On the other hand, love, communication, family, nurturing, and harmony are regularly understood as female. (Even modern bestsellers such as *Men Are from Mars, Women Are from Venus* follow this line.[2])

So please don't judge me when I use *feminine* to describe

the soft virtues and *masculine* to describe the hard ones. The purpose of this book is not to stereotype. Nor am I assigning certain traits to males and others to females. Quite the opposite. My prayer is that men and women will develop both sides of their personalities. I'm pleading with women to be strong, and with men to embrace weakness. My labels may not be PC, but they're instantly understandable.

Once again, here are the three journeys of Jesus, and where they're found:

- Matthew 1–7: the journey of submission
- Matthew 8–25: the journey of strength
- Matthew 26–28: the journey of sacrifice

As you read through these passages, you may notice the divisions between them are not absolutely rigid. Contained in each journey are a few verses that don't quite fit the pattern. For example, smack in the middle of the journey of submission, Jesus shouts, "Repent, for the kingdom of heaven is near" (4:17). There's also a brief mention of healing powers and battles with demons. These attributes belong in the journey of strength, yet Matthew gives them a nod during the journey of submission.

Other verses seem a bit out of place. Perhaps the most obvious occurs at the end of Matthew 10–11. Christ spends these two chapters in the thick of strength. Here we see a full-mane Lion of Judah, promising persecution, betrayal, and death to his followers. He warns them, "I did not come to bring peace, but a sword" (10:34). He insults the crowd and pronounces woe on unrepentant cities. Then in the midst of this scorching desert of challenge, an oasis of comfort appears. Jesus coos, "Come to me, all you who are weary and burdened, and I will give you rest. Take my yoke upon you and learn from me, for I am gentle and humble in heart, and you will find rest for your souls. For my yoke is easy and my burden is light" (11:28–30). This soft, nurturing verse really belongs in the journey of submission. So why is it double-parked in the journey of strength?

Matthew is showing us that spiritual journeys are not like physical ones. A physical journey requires you to be in one place at a time, but a spiritual journey might not. Confused? Here's an illustration that might help.

PHYSICAL JOURNEY (LINEAR)

You're driving a car from Phoenix to El Paso. You begin your journey in Arizona. Then you cross the border into New Mexico. Finally, you enter Texas, where your journey ends. You move sequentially from one state to another, occupying only one state at a time, except for that brief moment when you pass from one state to the next. When you are in Arizona, you are *not* in Texas, and vice versa.

SPIRITUAL JOURNEY (NONLINEAR)

Vic is a young believer who has only known the Lord for a week. Even though he has barely submitted anything to God yet, he senses the Spirit empowering him to share his faith with one of his old drinking buddies. He's clearly in his journey of submission, yet the Lord is calling him to do something strong.

Of course, Vic may go overboard and start telling every

person he meets about Christ, regardless of whether he's being led by the Spirit. Everyone has heard stories of young Christians who are so "on fire for Jesus" they become obnoxious. These inexperienced evangelists often bring discredit to the name of Christ, because they pursue a journey of strength before the proper time. A period of submission must come first. This is why the Bible prohibits recent converts from becoming elders (1 Timothy 3:6). A man cannot consistently walk in strength until he possesses a firm foundation of submission—no exceptions.

Here's another mystery: unlike a physical journey, you never fully complete a spiritual journey. A wise Christian would never say, "Whew. I'm done with submission. Glad to have that over with." Submission is not a class we complete but an attitude we absorb. You submit to God anew every morning, but over time submission is supposed to become second nature.

On the other hand, just because you never fully complete a spiritual journey doesn't mean you're to remain fixated on it the rest of your life. The purpose of the Christian life is not to make you submit. Cowboys don't break the same horse every day for ten years. Soldiers don't spend their military careers in basic training. Mountaineers don't waste a clear, calm day sitting at base camp. Submission is the root system of the Christian life, not its mighty trunk.

Still confused? I know—you're used to thinking of journeys in physical terms. Perhaps another illustration will help: Think about your grandfather's life. He probably walked three vocational journeys, in this order: *education*, *employment*, and *retirement*. This is generally how life plays out: you learn, you do, and you retire.

However, in real life, the journeys overlap somewhat, especially in the modern world. I began my journey of education at age five, when I enrolled in kindergarten. But even as a young man I began dabbling in employment: mowing lawns, walking neighbors' dogs, and holding summer jobs as a teen. In high school I worked at a bookstore sixteen hours a week. As a senior in college I was working several jobs to pay my tuition. So even in the midst of my journey of education, I was beginning my journey of employment.

At age twenty-two, I graduated from college and landed my first career-track job. My journey of education officially ended, and my journey of employment began. I was no longer a student; I was a worker. But I kept learning. I took some classes. I got training. I acquired knowledge from experienced professionals in my field. Retirement promises to be even messier. I might go back to school, or I may work until the day I die. Who knows?

Here's my point: the three journeys of Jesus are less like a cross-country automobile trip and more like a vocation. The divisions between them are not cut-and-dried. However, there is a regular order to them. Nobody retires at age sixteen. Rarely do seventy-year-olds train for a new career. So it is with our inner lives: there is room for some variation, but any man who would become great will walk the three journeys in their proper order. We leave the details to God. He reserves the right to teach whatever lesson he wants—whenever he wants.

You may look at the gospel of Matthew and say, "Three journeys? I don't see them. Murrow is imagining things." If that is your opinion, I disagree. There is strong evidence that the three journeys exist, and that Matthew intended for us to find them.

1. IT FOLLOWS COMMON JEWISH PRACTICE

Remember my fictional conversation with Gerasimos about the Jewish roots of Matthew's gospel? This is actually true. Bible scholars are unanimous in their belief that Matthew had a Hebrew audience in mind when he wrote his gospel. And Jewish writers were known to embed codes, patterns, and numbers into their writings to illuminate the text. So it's no stretch to posit that Matthew might have inserted the path of male discipleship into his account, albeit in code.

2. IT MATCHES WHAT WE KNOW OF MATTHEW'S ACCOUNT

Many Bible experts also believe that Matthew's gospel is not a chronological, blow-by-blow account of Jesus' earthly ministry.[3] If this is true, then why did Matthew choose to tell the story in the order he did? I believe that the author of this gospel (under the inspiration of the Holy Spirit) was trying to show us something important by choosing this specific chronology.

3. MATTHEW IS THE ONLY GOSPEL TO REVEAL JESUS' PERSONALITY IN THREE SUBDIVISIONS

Mark and John completely ignore the journey of submission. They both portray a strong Jesus right out of the starting gate. In John's gospel, Christ starts strong but seems to soften over time. In John 2 Jesus is overturning tables, but by chapter 11 he's weeping openly. John devotes almost half his gospel to the journey of sacrifice, beginning with Jesus' anointing in John 12.

Luke's account is a bit closer to Matthew's in chronology, but he mixes submitted Jesus and strong Jesus together indiscriminately. In Luke 6 the Lord blesses the poor, hungry, weeping, and persecuted, but in the following verses he curses the rich, well fed, happy, and popular. In Luke 19 Christ weeps over Jerusalem, but moments later he's swinging a whip and destroying stuff.

Bottom line: unlike the other gospel writers, Matthew took great care to present the life of Jesus in three separate acts. The first and last journeys are characterized by powerlessness and humility. The middle journey is imbued with strength and confidence. It seems obvious that Matthew *chose* to reveal Christ's ministry and personality as a series of three journeys.

Still don't believe me? Then consider this: the three journeys are also evident in the lives of the greatest men of the Old and New Testaments. Those men who walked the three journeys became great. And those who didn't? They were annihilated. Destroyed. Wiped out. *Gulp.*

We'll meet four of these Bible greats in our next chapter. Men who followed the map—and men who went another way.

Chapter 12

THE WAY
OF ALL GREAT MEN

It's not just Jesus who walked the three journeys. As you study the giants of Scripture, you'll see the pattern repeated over and over. Those men who walked the journeys in order (submission, strength, sacrifice) became powerful, influential men who finished well. But those who deviated paid a steep price. Here are four examples.

MOSES

Raised in Pharaoh's court, Moses is a golden boy who has been given every advantage. One day he sees an Egyptian beating a fellow Hebrew. So he reacts to this challenge like a typical man: he tackles it in his own strength, killing the Egyptian and hiding the body. At this moment, Moses is standing on the manly foothills.

But word gets around, and soon Moses is wanted for murder. He must flee for his life. Thus begins his journey of submission. Moses spends years exiled in the desert, stripped of his power, wealth, and influence. His home is no longer a palace but a tent. He spends his days in the company of sheep and goats, instead of wise men and philosophers. (Hint: Anytime you see a Bible character wandering in the desert, he is on the journey of submission. Even the nation of Israel did its time in the sand.)

One day the Lord decides this man has been humbled enough. He speaks to Moses from a burning bush and commands him to remove his shoes (a final sign of submission). Then God calls Moses to a specific journey of strength: to rescue the nation of Israel from the grip of Pharaoh.

Moses reacts like a typical man who has been walking in submission for forty years: he refuses his journey of strength. "No way, God!" he says, and he serves up a variety of excuses. But the Lord won't let him off the hook. Eventually Moses accepts the call, screws up his courage, and marches into the presence of Pharaoh. The journey of strength has begun. You know what happens next: plagues, Passover, and parting of the sea. Moses quickly grows from a humble shepherd into a mighty liberator, leader, and lawgiver.

Moses' journey of sacrifice begins just as God is preparing to give the Ten Commandments. We find Moses walking in strength, serving as the people's lone judge. He's working long hours and he's exhausted. This is one of the hazards of the journey of strength: thinking it all depends on me, me, me.

Fortunately for Moses, his father-in-law happens to be in town. The wise old man takes Moses aside and says:

> You will need to appoint some competent leaders who respect God and are trustworthy and honest. Then put them over groups of ten, fifty, a hundred, and a thousand. These judges can handle the ordinary cases and bring the

more difficult ones to you. Having them to share the load
will make your work easier. (Exodus 18:21–22 CEV)

Moses takes his father-in-law's advice. He stops trying to
do everything himself and begins developing other men into
leaders (Deuteronomy 1:16–17). Instead of jealously guarding all power for himself, he sacrifices some of it, pouring it
into competent, wise men—just as Jesus would someday do
with his disciples.

Moses' final days are the perfect picture of sacrifice. He calls
the people together and publicly taps Joshua as his successor
(Deuteronomy 31:1–8). This is no last-minute appointment;
Moses had groomed Joshua for this role since he was a lad
(Numbers 11:28). Moses blesses the twelve tribes, climbs to
the top of a mountain, stands at its peak, and dies.

Oh yeah! That's the way to go out—on top. Unfortunately,
that's not how our next Bible hero ends his days on earth.

DAVID

The youngest son of Jesse is a humble shepherd. He has
no royal aspirations. One day the prophet Samuel summons the boy and anoints him king. But David doesn't
assume power right away. Instead, he humbly submits to the
authority of the reigning monarch, Saul. David becomes a
musician in Saul's court, and he goes on to defeat a giant
with a slingshot.

But Saul becomes jealous as David's star rises. Saul tries
to kill his protégé several times. David repeatedly walks the
journey of submission by refusing to take Saul's life, even
when he's given golden opportunities to do so. This is the
Old Testament's finest picture of submission. David will not

seize power; instead, he patiently waits for the Lord to give it to him.

After Saul's death, David's journey of strength begins in earnest. He takes the throne, consolidates power, and unites Israel and Judah under his reign. He wins a series of military campaigns and brings peace to the land. Then the Lord promises to make his name great, a name that will endure forever. He is at the peak of his strength, yet he has not forgotten the lessons of submission (2 Samuel 7:18–29).

David is well on his way to conquering the mountain of manhood. But then his train starts to run off the rails. The king continues to pile up military victories, but eventually success wearies him. So he sends his generals out to fight the battles while he stays home. After sleeping the day away, the bored king spies a beautiful woman named Bathsheba, the wife of Uriah, one of his soldiers. He summons her to his bedchamber and seduces her. She becomes pregnant. David eventually plots Uriah's murder and takes Bathsheba as another wife. God is not pleased. The prophet Nathan exposes David's sin to the nation; the tabloids are abuzz.

The scandal weakens David politically. His family spins out of control: rape, murder, and rebellion strike repeatedly at him and his loved ones. David's thirdborn son, Absalom, attempts a coup d'état. Son tries to kill father, but the young rebel is himself killed, grieving David greatly. Near the end of his reign, David is so despondent he doesn't even defend himself when mockers throw rocks at him and his men. (Note the irony: the man who slew Goliath with a stone is now on the receiving end.)

One day David is near death. He's a pitiful shell of his former self: weak, bedridden, and lying next to a virgin to keep him warm. In the streets another rival proclaims himself king. A desperate Bathsheba storms into David's bedchamber and reminds him of his promise to place Solomon on the throne. Finally, David makes a much-belated attempt at the third journey. He hands the kingdom over to Bathsheba's son. He speaks a blessing over Solomon and dies, not on a mountain peak, but in bed, shivering next to a young girl.

David made it two-thirds of the way up the mountain, but he got lost during the final ascent. The nation of Israel paid a terrible price for David's refusal to complete his three journeys.

PAUL

Born Saul, he's a high-achieving alpha male who studied under Israel's top rabbi. Saul is unsurpassed in his zeal for the Jewish law and describes himself as a Hebrew among Hebrews (Philippians 3:5).

The first time Saul is mentioned in Scripture, he's a young man learning the art of religiously motivated violence. He plays the role of coat-check boy at the stoning of Stephen. One chapter later he's rounding up Christians and signing their death warrants.

At this point, Saul is standing on a blood-soaked foothill called religious fanaticism. He honestly believes he's doing the right thing. Saul's preconversion life is a perfect illustration of the damage a sincere man can inflict when his heart is not submitted to a loving God.

One day Saul is marching down the road to Damascus, "breathing threats and murder against the disciples of the Lord," when a light flashes from heaven (Acts 9:1 ESV). Saul falls to the ground and is suddenly rendered blind (a metaphor for his spiritual condition). Then he hears the voice of Christ telling him to go to Damascus and await his orders. Saul faces a moment of decision: he can submit to Jesus, or he can remain in darkness the rest of his life.

Saul begins the journey of submission. He obeys. He prays. He fasts. But he's still blind. He needs the help of another man to regain his sight. So the Lord speaks to Ananias, a mature disciple.

Hey, Ananias?

"Yes, Lord?"

You know Saul, that guy who's been killing all my followers? Go lay hands on him. Then he will see.

Understandably, Ananias questions his orders, fearing for his life. But he does as he's told. Do you see the bigger picture here? This is a brilliant illustration of an experienced follower conquering his own fear in order to approach a dangerous, wild bull of a man who needs the touch of God.

Back to Saul. He surrenders his life to Jesus. With all his theological training, you'd think he'd breeze through the journey of submission. Not so fast. The former persecutor of Christians spends the first three years of his faith walk stuck in the Arabian Desert (remember: desert = submission). Then he returns to Damascus and tries his hand at preaching, but the time isn't right. Within a few weeks he's fleeing for his life. He retreats to the region of Tarsus for a period of time, perhaps years. All the while, God is teaching him to submit. Eventually he is summoned to Antioch and begins doing a little teaching there. His journey of submission is almost complete.

Saul is finally sent on his first missionary journey. He quickly encounters a false prophet named Bar-Jesus who is trying to turn the Roman proconsul away from the faith. Here is what Saul says[1] to this blasphemer:

"You son of the devil, you enemy of all righteousness, full of all deceit and villainy, will you not stop making crooked the straight paths of the Lord? And now, behold, the hand of the Lord is upon you, and you will be blind and unable to see the sun for a time." Immediately mist and darkness fell upon him, and he went about seeking people to lead him by the hand. (Acts 13:10–11 ESV)

Harsh words? Prophetic warning? His first recorded miracle? Looks to me like Saul's journey of strength has finally begun. And just to be sure you didn't miss the transition, from this point forward he's never again referred to as Saul. The name is *Paul*, thank you very much.

This new Paul is an unstoppable train. His journey of strength is legendary. He becomes history's greatest evangelist and church father. Only Christ himself accomplished more during the second journey.

Paul throws himself into the third journey as well. He trains no fewer than a dozen men to carry on his work, taking them on his missionary journeys and teaching them by example.[2] Paul remains faithful to the end and was probably martyred for his faith. The apostle Paul is a powerful example of what a man can accomplish when he completes all three journeys.

SAMSON

What happens when a Bible hero skips the journeys altogether? Read the account of Samson in Judges 13–16. Samson is a vengeful, violent, spoiled brat. He takes whatever he wants, and he kills whoever or whatever gets in his way. He's physically strong but spiritually feeble.

One day Samson makes a foolish wager and loses. What does this strongman do? He murders thirty innocent men and strips their still-warm corpses of clothing to pay his debt. After spending the night with a prostitute, he rips down the city gates with his bare hands in order to escape capture. He gets mad at his Philistine father-in-law, and his lust for revenge ignites a war that kills thousands.

Samson is the classic alpha male who spends his life standing on the manly foothills, blasting away with his power, leaving craters of human suffering. He may look strong on the outside, but he is only pretending to conquer his mountain. In reality, he is on no journey at all.

Men like Samson always meet a tragic end. The Philistines finally discover the truth: Samson's awesome strength will disappear if his hair is cut. So as the mighty one sleeps, the Philistines call in a barber. They subdue Samson and pluck out his eyes. Powerless, blind, and shackled, Samson is tortured before an audience of three thousand Philistines, who hurl down curses at him. In this most desperate moment, Samson finally submits to God: he prays in humility that his strength will return. God gives him back his power, and he uses it to topple the building, killing more Philistines than he ever had before (Judges 16:30).

See what happened? Samson submitted; he gained his strength, and he sacrificed himself for his people. He walked all three journeys in the final two minutes of his life.

Men, you will walk the three journeys—whether you choose to or not. The only question is, are you going to work with God, or against him?

Many other men of the Bible also walked the three journeys. If you discover one, drop me a line at www.threejourneys.com.

Chapter 13

THE JOURNEY
OF SUBMISSION

I like to keep a tidy garage. But on this particular day it looked like the French Quarter the morning after Mardi Gras.

In the midst of the chaos stood two bearded young men. They were unloading and reloading their backpacks, preparing for an assault on Mount McKinley, North America's highest peak. The mountaineers were staying at our home in Chugiak, Alaska, waiting for good weather so an air taxi could lift them to base camp on Kahiltna Glacier.

They had divided their provisions into three piles: must take, might take, and probably won't take. The climbers built their piles with the utmost care: Carry too much weight up the mountain and they'd never reach the summit. Bring too little and they could lose life or limb. The adventurers agonized over each decision, because there's no place to pick up an extra pair of gloves on the brutal flanks of McKinley.

In mountaineering terms, the journey of submission is like emptying your pack of everything that weighs you down. It means unpacking your life; taking a good, hard look at what you find; and leaving behind those things that might keep you from reaching the summit. Only a fool would lug a heavy can of beef stew up the mountain when a lightweight, freeze-dried alternative exists. In the same way, we will never make it up the mountain of manhood loaded down with self-ishness, pride, independence, and earthly wisdom. We must allow God to replace our heavy burdens with his lightweight alternatives (Matthew 11:30).

It just occurred to me that some of you might dislike the word *submission*. It may suggest oppression, subservience, or even violence. I searched for another term that was less likely to offend, but no single word so accurately captures the theme of our early walk with Christ.

Although submission may seem out of style, we humans submit willingly all the time. In fact, we find fulfillment only when we submit to benevolent authority. Athletes win championships when they submit to their coaches. Students learn when they submit to their teachers. Societies find peace and order when citizens submit to civil authorities. Businesses prosper when employees submit to management. Believers are instructed to submit to one another out of reverence for Christ (Ephesians 5:21). In the absence of voluntary submission, there can be no personal growth—only a selfish autonomy.

Before we examine Jesus' journey of submission as recorded in Matthew's gospel, quickly recall Gerasimos's metaphors for this journey:

- ***Driving the direction you don't want to go.*** Submission is difficult because it means moving away from masculinity, as most men define it.
- ***Breaking the horse.*** Submission is the painful process

of learning to obey our new master—to grant him ultimate control over our wills.

- *The foundation of the building.* Submission is the ground floor of our lives. It may not be something people notice, but it supports everything else.
- *The seed.* As we learn to submit, our human will is like a seed that dies and falls into the ground. Eventually it grows into something big and powerful (John 12:24).

It's time to examine Jesus' journey of submission in detail. Along the way, we'll stop and have a look at seven points of interest. Since we're climbing a mountain, let's call them *trail markers*.

TRAIL MARKER 1: RELINQUISHING YOUR OWN POWER

We meet Christ not as a man, but as a baby, wrapped in swaddling clothes and lying in a manger. Yeah, yeah, yeah—we've all heard the Nativity story a thousand times before. But did you ever consider the huge risk God took by doing it this way?

Why didn't Christ arrive on Planet Earth as an adult? Angels always do. They show up fully mature, locked and loaded for mission. If I were Jesus, I'd have done it this way. Why not skip childhood and move right to doing miracles?

But our Lord chose a more difficult path. He came as a baby, in what we would call an at-risk pregnancy. His mother was an unwed teenager. He was born in a stable, the first-century equivalent of a parking lot. He was poor and homeless. The God of the universe was unable to feed, clothe, or protect himself.

Why would Jesus choose to enter our world in such a tiny, vulnerable, and impoverished package? To show us the first step in discipleship: *relinquishing our own power*. Jesus voluntarily forsook all the power in the universe in exchange for the humblest advent imaginable.

So what's the lesson for us? A man's journey up the mountain begins when he, like Christ, voluntarily relinquishes his own power. He must despise his own goodness, his own wisdom, and his own talent. He must "come to the end of himself" and realize that he is not captain of his own ship. (Twelve-step recovery programs begin this way: "We admitted we were powerless . . .")

One day a very earnest, wealthy, and clean-living young man came to Jesus and asked him what he must do to have life. Christ challenged this fellow to live by the commandments. In a shockingly self-confident reply, the young man said, "I have done so since I was a boy." Then the Master got to the heart of the matter:

> Jesus answered, "If you want to be perfect, go, sell your possessions and give to the poor, and you will have treasure in heaven. Then come, follow me."
>
> When the young man heard this, he went away sad, because he had great wealth.
>
> Then Jesus said to his disciples, "I tell you the truth, it is hard for a rich man to enter the kingdom of heaven. Again I tell you, it is easier for a camel to go through the eye of a needle than for a rich man to enter the kingdom of God." (Matthew 19:21–24)

I don't think Christ is saying that rich people are bound for hell, by virtue of their assets. Instead, Jesus is pointing out that it's often hard for the wealthy to experience the abundant life that his kingdom has to offer, because they depend so heavily upon their own power. Why lean on God's clout when you've got your own?

Just yesterday I was visiting a childhood friend I hadn't seen in decades. She has had cancer, a heart attack, and a stroke. She's in constant pain and depends on seventeen medications to maintain a modicum of health. She and her four-year-old adopted son live hand to mouth. She's too sick to work, but too well to receive much in disability payments. Her apartment is a wreck and smells of kitty litter. Yet this woman possesses something I don't: the gift of faith. My friend doesn't get through the day without minute-by-minute infusions of God's power.

I must admit I don't really know God this way. I don't wake up wondering how I'm going to make it through the day. It's been a long time since I've prayed, "Give us this day our daily bread"—and meant it. Strong, healthy, resourceful men often miss the first lesson of kingdom living because they do not understand powerlessness.

Now, please don't feel guilty for having health, food, or a few dollars in the bank. These are gifts, and God is happy for you to have them. But the first prayer of a disciple of Jesus should be this one: "How can I relinquish more of my power to you, God?" In the case of the rich young man, it meant giving up worldly wealth—in order to find true riches.

Tell me, how can you be a little less self-powered today?

TRAIL MARKER 2: DEPENDING ON GOD TO PROVIDE

Matthew is the only gospel writer to record the visit of the magi, or wise men. Why did he include this story when the others did not? To illustrate the second trail marker of submission: dependence on God.

Contrary to popular myth, the wise men were not present the night Christ was born. By the time they showed up in the region of Bethlehem, young Jesus was probably walking. The magi dropped in on a surprised Mary and Joseph and handed them three expensive gifts: gold, frankincense, and myrrh. I always wondered why a toddler would need these costly items. A few verses later, the answer is revealed.

After the magi departed, Joseph was warned in a dream to bundle up his family and flee to Egypt, because King Herod was planning to kill Jesus. That very night, Joseph, Mary, and Jesus fled. Tell me, how did this impoverished couple finance such an expensive journey (without a fourteen-day advance purchase)? Well, they happened to have a nice stash of gold, frankincense, and myrrh. God had provided in the nick of time—out of the blue.

As followers of Jesus, we may be powerless, but we are not without power. The second lesson of discipleship is this: rely on God to meet your needs. Andrew Murray said, "God is ready to assume full responsibility for the life wholly yielded to Him."[1] This axiom is not a license to live recklessly but an invitation to depend more fully on God (and his people) for our provision.

TRAIL MARKER 3: SUBMITTING TO THE RULES

The next time Matthew presents Jesus, he's a grown man who has not yet started his ministry. His cousin, John the Baptist, is a fiery prophet, preaching and baptizing on the banks of the Jordan River.

Then Jesus came from Galilee to the Jordan to be baptized by John. But John tried to deter him, saying, "I need to be baptized by you, and do you come to me?"

Jesus replied, "Let it be so now; it is proper for us to do this to fulfill all righteousness." Then John consented. (3:13–15)

Jesus agrees with John: there's no need to baptize the Son of God. Christ has no sins to be cleansed. Sinful John baptizing holy Jesus? It's kind of like a first-time golfer offering a few putting tips to Tiger Woods.

Yet Christ insists on going through with baptism in order to "fulfill all righteousness." In other words, Jesus is willing to submit himself to the rules and to jump through a few religious hoops, even though they don't apply to him.

I have not always been this humble. One time I moved to a new city and began attending a church in the same denomination as my old one. My new congregation offered a six-week "Inquirer's Class" as a prelude to membership. I was frustrated by this requirement—what was the point? I'd been a Christian for many years and was well versed in our denominational polity. I had recently taken a similar class at my previous church. So for years I attended church but never joined, because I didn't want to jump through this hoop. Finally, I went so far as to study the denomination's constitution in order to find an alternate path to membership.

I look back on this episode with shame. Yes, maybe the great and powerful David Murrow had little to gain from another membership class. Perhaps it would have been a waste of my precious time. But in hindsight I realize that I flunked a test from the Lord. I refused an opportunity to "fulfill all righteousness." I blew a chance to humble myself and submit to the elders of my new congregation. Who knows, I might have learned something, met a lifelong friend, or had an opportunity to encourage a fellow inquirer.

This kind of pride is rampant among Christians today. We have millions who have forsaken Christian fellowship because they can't find a church where they "feel comfortable." If their pastor says something they disagree with, it's off to find a new church. Others won't obey the standards of their congregation and are offended when they don't get a personal exemption from the rules. These so-called Christians are happy to follow Jesus as long as they retain total control of their spiritual formation.

TRAIL MARKER 4: RECEIVING GOD'S LOVE AND ACCEPTANCE

Next, Matthew tells us:

> As soon as Jesus was baptized, he went up out of the water. At that moment heaven was opened, and he saw the Spirit of God descending like a dove and lighting on him. And a voice from heaven said, "This is my Son, whom I love; with him I am well pleased." (3:16–17)

Speaker Jamie Lash tells a funny story that illustrates the Father's great love for his children. The angels Gabriel and Michael are standing in the break room of heaven, sipping coffee. Suddenly, God shows up.

GABRIEL. Uh-oh, here comes the Father . . .
MICHAEL. Quick, hide!
GOD. Oh, there you are, guys. Have you seen my

kids? [God pulls out an enormous wallet, with
photos spilling onto the ground.] This is Shane
from Australia—what a great guy. And here's Greta
from Germany; I am crazy about her. Then there's
Wolde in Ethiopia; he's one of my favorites. And
Marisela from Nicaragua—I'm so proud of her!

GABRIEL. Uh, God, we've got to be running
along . . .

GOD. Hang on, I've only got 760 million more to
show you.[2]

This little parable is not meant to portray God as a heavenly bore, but to illustrate how much he loves his kids. He
is crazy about you. Really. He's not mad at you. You are not
a screw-up or a disappointment. His only emotion toward
his children is love. When God looks at you, he sees you the
same way he sees Jesus: *This is my Son, whom I love; with him
I am well pleased.*

Sometimes it's hard for a man to believe that God loves
him so much. A lot of guys never received much love from
their earthly fathers, so it's hard for them to imagine a heavenly Father who cares so deeply for his sons. But it's true.
Regardless of what you have done (or may still be doing),
if you've asked Jesus to be your Savior, then God is carrying your photo in his wallet. The Bible is clear: "There is
now no condemnation for those who are in Christ Jesus"
(Romans 8:1).

When I ask my adult son to do me a favor, I want him to
do it out of love—not because he feels fear, guilt, or obligation. And so it is with God. He doesn't want men serving him
out of a sense of duty or debt or even out of a fear of hell. In
fact, God is not interested in great acts of faith, unless they

are motivated by love. The apostle Paul tells us, "If I give all I possess to the poor and surrender my body to the flames, but have not love, I gain nothing" (1 Corinthians 13:3).

The most destructive churchmen are those who do not know the love of God. They know the routines, the rules, and all the verses of all the songs—but they don't know God's great love personally. Such men will never conquer the mountain of manhood.

Men, don't be afraid to receive God's love and acceptance. I've seen many a tough guy reduced to a blubbering mess the moment he realizes how much God loves him. That's okay. Remember, the journey of submission moves us in the feminine direction. Just let the tears come. You'll return to the masculine side of the mountain soon enough.

TRAIL MARKER 5: FIGHTING FROM A POSITION OF WEAKNESS

One of my favorite films is *Rocky*. Not *Rocky II, III, IV, V,* or *Balboa*—the original. Remember the famous training scene with the raw eggs, the one-handed push-ups, the cow carcass punching bag, and finally, the triumphant run up the steps as the background singers warble, "Getting Strong Now"? Rocky was doing what prizefighters do: strengthening himself before a big fight.

You would think Jesus might do the same before his title bout with the prince of darkness. But no—he intentionally weakened himself. Here's how Matthew describes the Messiah's prefight workout: "Then Jesus was led by the Spirit into the desert to be tempted by the devil. After fasting forty days and forty nights, he was hungry" (4:1–2).

Christ, facing creation's most dangerous foe, made himself

physically frail. No food. Little water. Merciless sun. Isolation. Loneliness. Is this any way to prepare for a fight?

Christ underwent this counterintuitive training regimen to show us another important truth: in the spiritual world, we are most effective not when we are strong but when we are weak. Only in our weakness does God's power flow through us.

There was a time when the apostle Paul was suffering terribly. He prayed that God would relieve his torment, but God said to him, "My kindness is all you need. My power is strongest when you are weak" (2 Corinthians 12:9 CEV).

Years ago, my youngest daughter, Shea, and her best friend, Rachel, were struggling to open a jar of strawberry jam. They worked on that lid for ten minutes, but their five-year-old hands just couldn't break the seal. Then I walked into the kitchen. Shea handed me the jar. Not only did I open it for her, but I also whipped up two of my award-winning peanut-butter-and-jelly sandwiches.

Here's the lesson: the more we use our own strength to fight our battles, to provide for our own needs, and to feather our own nests, the less God's strength flows through us. We have unlimited power at our disposal, if only we'll hand the jar to God.

Now back to the boxing match. In the far corner we have the undisputed heavyweight champion of the world, the prince of darkness. In the near corner, we have Jesus, physically weak but spiritually strong. The bell rings and the devil lands three punches—a trio of temptations. Each time Christ deflects the blows. How? By using the Bible. When the tempter whispers in his ear, Jesus doesn't think up some clever reply. He simply quotes the Scriptures. In other words, he allows God's Word to do the fighting for him.

Men, the next time life is spinning out of control or temptations rage, fight the way Jesus did—from a position of weakness. Get away and pray. Fast. Counterpunch with the words of the Bible. There are so many things about life you can't control (if you doubt this, adopt a teenager). Whatever battle you are fighting right now, take a moment to give it to God. Search Scripture for an answer. Don't rely on your own strength, but get it from God. It only takes a minute to hand him the jar.

TRAIL MARKER 6: GATHERING A TEAM

Once Jesus defeats the tempter, he returns home and then moves to Capernaum, where he begins preaching. His first order of business, though, is to assemble a band of disciples. He calls twelve men who will be his constant companions for the next three years.

Here is Matthew's lesson: you cannot make a solo ascent of the mountain of manhood. You need climbing partners to go with you. Christianity is—and always has been—a team sport. Jesus never sent anyone out alone.

Yet because of the way our modern society and our congregations are structured, men tend to become isolated, even in church. A Gallup poll of churchgoers found that 51 percent of women had a best friend in their congregation, while only 35 percent of men did.[3] Dan Erickson writes, "Even in the church, very few men have close friends. For the most part, men are spiritually fed but relationally bankrupt.[4]

Lions are wise hunters. They don't attack the herd; they strike the animal that's off on its own, separated from the group. Go-it-alone types make an easy meal.

So it is in the spiritual world. The apostle Peter writes,

"Your enemy the devil prowls around like a roaring lion looking for someone to devour" (1 Peter 5:8). The evil one is an experienced hunter who always stalks the man who's far from the herd.

Men, if you are isolated, you are easy prey. It's not enough to go to church on Sundays; you need a small group of guys you really know and trust. Guys you meet with regularly. Guys who can help you get up the mountain. I'm not talking about a couples' Bible study; I mean guys. Why just men? Go read Matthew 10:2–4. How many women do you see in Jesus' inner circle? Any couples? Children?

TRAIL MARKER 7: THE SERMON ON THE MOUNT (MATTHEW 5–7)

"The Sermon on the Mount" is a poor name for the greatest sermon ever preached. It tells us nothing more than the location where Jesus stood as he spoke. A far better title would be "The Sermon on Submission." No single word better captures the theme, content, and tone of Jesus' world-changing discourse.

Consider the sermon's greatest passages: *Blessed are the meek. Blessed are the poor in spirit. Blessed are the peacemakers. Do not resist an evil person. Love your enemy. Turn the other cheek. Do not judge. Do unto others as you would have them do unto you.* Christ called these would-be disciples to a radical weakness. A holy passivity. An others-first humility.

Jesus' call to weakness and submission stood in stark contrast to the religion of his day. First-century Judaism had devolved into a harshly masculine faith: controlling, legalistic, and performance based. The God of the Pharisees offered wrath, not acceptance. He was a feared overlord, not a loving father. Perhaps this was to be expected: after centuries of domination by outsiders, Judaism was a religion that sought power, fought back, and took revenge.

Yet Jesus stood on that mountainside and laid out a very different path to freedom. Christ was clearly pushing these inexperienced disciples in the direction all men must go as they begin their faith journeys—toward a softer spiritual posture.

Some have suggested that the Sermon on the Mount is a comprehensive guide to discipleship. I disagree. It's Christianity 101—delivered to people who have never heard the good news. It's an overview of Christianity's basic, ground-floor truths. Jesus tells us so. Look at how he concludes his sermon:

> "Therefore everyone who hears these words of mine and puts them into practice is like a wise man who built his house on the rock. The rain came down, the streams rose, and the winds blew and beat against that house; yet it did not fall, because it had its foundation on the rock. But everyone who hears these words of mine and does not put them into practice is like a foolish man who built his house on sand. The rain came down, the streams rose, and the winds blew and beat against that house, and it fell with a great crash." (7:24–27)

Do you see it? Jesus is making a direct comparison between "these words of mine" (the sermon he just preached) and the foundation of a building. In other words, the Sermon on the Mount is *foundational truth*. It's the bottom layer of your spiritual life. Submission, weakness, humility, and dependence on God—these form a strong base that will hold fast when the storms of life blow.

But submission is not everything. The Christian life is

not about turning ourselves into meek, gentle doormats who lose every fight and cry at the drop of a hankie.

Your goal is to live a life of submission to Christ without becoming *submissive*. You will draw men and women to Christ by living a life of strength, rooted in an underlying humility. *Submissive* is not the first word that should come to people's lips when they describe you, as in, "Wow, that Murrow is such a submissive, weak, and dependent guy. He's so in touch with his feminine side."

Jesus made it clear: submission is merely the substructure. There is still a house to be built. As men who follow Jesus, we cannot stop at the foundation; we must raise the rest of the house—or everyone will suffer (Luke 14:28–30).

So the sermon ends. Jesus descends and everything changes. "Gentle Jesus, meek and mild" disappears, and a new Christ takes his place. We'll meet this startling Savior in our next chapter.

Chapter 14

THE JOURNEY
OF STRENGTH

Strength is the second journey of Jesus. The Christ revealed in chapters 8–25 of Matthew's gospel bears little resemblance to the helpless babe we met in the hay. The man who declared, "Blessed are the meek," is now anything but. He who taught, "Love your enemies," suddenly finds himself surrounded by them. And how does he show his enemies love? By plunking them with rebukes, curses, and put-downs.

Such is the journey of strength. At times, it doesn't look much like "good Christian behavior." It's probably the least understood of the journeys. It always attracts opposition and criticism. But this is the journey that expands the kingdom of God on earth. The risks of the second journey are great, but so are its potential rewards.

Here's a great irony: the journey of strength moves a man in the masculine direction—yet many church-going men avoid this journey altogether. Richard Rohr is a Roman Catholic theologian who noticed this early in his career. As a young priest, Rohr served the New Jerusalem community in Cincinnati. This lay community was brimming with young couples raising children. Rohr taught repeatedly on the importance of conversion and surrender to God. He writes:

> In terms of masculinity and femininity, I was talking about conversion from male attitudes of autonomy and control to more feminine attitudes of relationship and trust. At that time I saw the whole Christian journey in those terms because, quite frankly, that's where I was as a young priest in my own spiritual development. . . .
>
> As a group, then, the community moved in the direction of more feminine attitudes and living styles. We were all into listening and acceptance and affirmation and dialogue both at the community level and in families. The young men discovered a whole new world opening up for them . . . they became very loving and nurturing fathers, quite different from many of the fathers they had grown up with.

So far so good. Rohr continues:

> But gradually we began to hear about all sorts of problems arising in the homes as the children grew older. Slowly it dawned on us that part of the problem was that the children were being raised by two mothers, so to speak. The children had no experience of a strong masculine presence in the home.
>
> Now, it's one thing for a man to get into his feminine side, but it's quite another to stay there—which is apparently what many of the young men in New Jerusalem were doing. No one could blame them, of course, because no

one had ever told them that at some point their spiritual journey had to take a different turn.[1]

Richard Rohr could have been describing me in this story. After I gave my life to Christ, my heart began moving in the feminine direction. I became softer. Gentler. More loving. After a few years I became so comfortable on the left flank of the mountain that I pitched my tent there and stocked it with love, caution, eternal security, and false humility. I became uneasy with men who were bold and aggressive. I was becoming what author Paul Coughlin calls "a Christian Nice Guy."[2] One day I read the parable of the talents. Jesus praised two servants who had doubled the funds entrusted to them— but he cursed the one who played it safe.

I took a hard look at my faith walk. God had invested heavily in me. Was my life producing a return worthy of his trust? I had to admit the answer was no. Church had taught me to play defense. I'd learned how *not* to sin, how *not* to hurt people's feelings, and how to smile pleasantly at potluck dinners. Christianity was a moral code that helped me order my world and keep my family safe. It lent a holy stamp of approval to my risk-averse personality.

But I was not strong—not in the way Jesus was strong. The kingdom of God was not "forcefully advancing" through my life (Matthew 11:12). In that moment I knew it was time to turn a corner. I needed to move back in the direction that I had been fleeing since I had submitted to Christ. I'd done a fine job getting in touch with my feminine side—but the time had come to reapproach my masculine side. And it scared me to death.

Here are Gerasimos's metaphors for the journey of strength:

- *Driving the direction you want to go*. This journey moves us in a classic masculine direction.
- *Working the horse*. The journey of strength is active. It's the "doing" and "accomplishing" era of your faith walk.
- *The walls of the building*. Your foundation (submission) has been laid. Strength is the aspect of your personality that you want others to notice.
- *The tree*. The seed you planted in submission is now growing into a tree of strength.

———

Before we begin looking at trail markers, here are two observations about this second journey.

THE JOURNEY OF STRENGTH IS THE LONGEST

In terms of raw word count, the second journey dwarfs the first and third. Matthew devotes about two-thirds of his gospel to strength.

A quick glance at the map might lead a man to believe the bulk of his spiritual life is supposed to move him in the feminine direction (two feminine journeys versus one masculine journey). But that's not true. Strength is the dominant journey. Since Matthew spent most of his gospel describing Jesus' journey of strength, we can assume that strength is supposed to be our "big" journey. The Lord wants his sons to begin the second journey as soon as possible—and to walk in strength for as long as they can.

THE JOURNEY OF STRENGTH
IS THE WILDEST

Matthew 8–25 contains all the action-packed stories you remember from Sunday school. Christ's abilities go from impressive to fantastic. No longer content to simply cast out demons, Christ sends them into pigs that commit mass suicide. His miracles become (I don't know how else to say this) *flashy*—walking on water, transfiguring before his disciples' eyes, and feeding thousands out of a single lunch bucket. His verbal duels with the Pharisees escalate. He enters Jerusalem to thunderous applause and then picks up a whip and drives the riffraff out of the temple. His final teachings sizzle with prophetic zeal.

Matthew is contrasting the peace and passivity of the first journey with the wildness and activity of the second. Here's what I mean: often when a man first submits his life to Christ, he experiences an initial period of turmoil; but over the weeks and months, his life calms down. Order replaces chaos as sin falls away. The new disciple experiences the serenity of a well-ordered existence. Some men stay in this safe zone—living a comfortable Christian life—the rest of their days.

But those who decide to turn the corner and begin the second journey will quickly see the wildness return to their lives. Whenever a man walks in strength, the forces of evil marshal to attack.

Jesus faced little direct human opposition during his first journey, but resistance increased as he moved through his second. You should expect the same.

The journey of strength is so significant in the gospel of Matthew (eighteen chapters and almost fifteen thousand words), I could devote an entire book to it. There are dozens of potential trail markers we could stop and inspect. But instead of focusing on the usual suspects, I'm going to point out six markers that portray a side of Jesus you may never have considered. Rather than looking at what Jesus did, we'll be examining *how* he did it. (You can download a detailed outline of all three journeys at www.threejourneys.com.)

TRAIL MARKER 1: POSSESSING MIRACULOUS POWER

The journey of strength starts off like a minefield of miracles—you can hardly read these early chapters without stepping on one. Jesus performs ten supernatural wonders in Matthew 8 and 9 alone.

Why is Christ in miracle overdrive as he commences his second journey? Matthew is showing us that when a man begins walking in strength, the first thing he should expect is power—the energy of heaven flowing through his life in wonderful, unexpected ways.

I remember the early stage of my journey of strength. Hardly a day went by without a miracle—big or small. At times it was almost laughable. I'd call my wife and say, "Honey, you'll never guess what happened today." Then I'd share a story that was impossible to explain apart from the intervention of God.

You may never heal a leper, battle a demon, or calm a storm. But understand this: when God's power flows through you, the universe changes. The natural slipstream of life is disrupted, and the goodness of God falls to earth. Anytime God's power flows through a man, it is a miracle.

TRAIL MARKER 2: BEING DEMANDING AND UNPLEASANT—TO FRIEND AND FOE

When pastors exhort us to "be like Jesus," they are not talking about the Christ of Matthew 8–25. Second-journey Jesus is not the gentle, beautiful Savior we sing about in church. The mid-gospel Christ is typically harsh, stern, and short-tempered.

In the midst of this journey, the Prince of Peace boldly declared, "Do not suppose that I have come to bring peace to the earth. I did not come to bring peace, but a sword" (Matthew 10:34). He reminded us that "the kingdom of heaven has been forcefully advancing, and forceful men lay hold of it" (11:12). He pronounced judgment on unrepentant cities (11:23) and seemed to go out of his way to be rude to the Pharisees.

When I was a young Christian, I used to enjoy reading those passages in which Jesus took his opponents out to the woodshed. But upon further study, I realized that Christ was pretty tough on his friends as well. He rebuked adoring crowds, calling them an "unbelieving and perverse generation" (17:17). When a disciple asked him to explain a parable, he shot back, "Are you being willfully stupid?" (15:16 MSG). Peter was foolish enough to question the Lord's plans, and Jesus erupted, "Get behind me, Satan! You are a stumbling block to me" (16:23).

Did you realize that Jesus was intentionally mean to the religious leaders? When the Pharisees asked him a question, he would often begin his reply this way: "Haven't you read the Scriptures?" This little dagger would have pierced the heart of a teacher of the law, who had spent decades studying every detail of the Torah. When Jesus says, "Haven't you read the Scriptures?" he's landing a low blow. On purpose. It's like saying to a professor of English literature, "You dummy. Haven't you read Shakespeare?"

So what are we to make of this? If God is love, then how can his Son be so mean?

Perhaps the problem lies not with Jesus but with our limited definition of love. As a man travels the journey of strength, he must learn to love in surprising ways—ways that may not *feel* very loving.

One of my favorite films is *Remember the Titans*. The story is set in the early 1970s, shortly after Virginia's public schools were forced to integrate. Herman Boone is hired as the first black football coach at T. C. Williams High School. He finds a team fractured along racial lines. Over the course of the season, Coach Boone helps the players overcome their prejudices and bond as brothers. The newly united Titans march all the way to the state championship game.

How was Boone able to achieve this miracle? Through gentleness? Tender mercy? Kind words? No, Boone was about as tender as a barbed-wire fence. He was impatient, demanding, and mean. I'm sure his boys didn't feel very loved as Coach Boone cut them down to size.

But there is no doubt: Coach Boone loved those boys. His harsh, challenging love led them to a football championship—and more importantly, to victory over prejudice and bigotry.

After my book *Why Men Hate Going to Church* became popular, I started meeting a number of famous ministry leaders. To my surprise, many of these men were not particularly friendly or warm. They were polite enough. But they weren't the kind of men who left you feeling good about yourself. They were often driven—even a bit acerbic. In fact, they reminded me of ambitious, type-A executives I'd met in the secular world.

At first I thought, *These men aren't really Christians! They don't have the Holy Spirit, because they sure aren't very loving.* But as I began studying the three journeys, I realized that Jesus was precisely this kind of man during his journey of strength.

I'm going to tell you something you'll never hear in church: You *can* fly into a rage and still be a faithful Christian. You can hurt people's feelings. You do not have to be *nice* all the time. You can say no to people. You can shut some people out. Jesus did all these things. And we are first and foremost imitators of Christ.

Just remember the cardinal rule of the journey of strength: do not forsake the lessons of submission. As long as you do everything out of love, and not out of bitterness, you can be demanding and even unpleasant once in a while—especially when dealing with other men.

TRAIL MARKER 3: EMBRACING TEACHINGS YOU MAY NOT PERSONALLY AGREE WITH

I wish there were no hell. I mean, if God is love, then how can he send anyone to eternal torment? Why can't everyone go to heaven and enjoy everlasting bliss? In my heart, I want to believe that everyone goes to heaven.

But that's not what Jesus taught. During his journey of strength, the Lord made it clear that in God's kingdom there are winners and losers. Some will enjoy eternal bliss, but others will be damned. Rewards accrue to the faithful, but punishment awaits the unfaithful. The Scriptures also indicate there will be inequality in heaven. Even among the elect, some will have more than others.[3] This disturbs me greatly.

So the Lord and I differ on this point (among others). What do I do about it? I believe what God tells me—and reject my own wisdom. I live as though the Bible is true and my own intellect is deceived. Even though I want to believe in universalism, I choose not to. I embrace the teachings of Scripture, though they offend me.

I can guarantee you this: as you read the Bible, you will encounter doctrines that bother you. You may disagree with teachings on marriage, money, sexuality, authority, and others. And Jesus' answer to you is: *So what? Who made you God?* Christ doesn't care about your opinion. He's God. You're not.

A weak man finds something he disagrees with in Scripture and says in his heart, *This can't be true, because it makes me uncomfortable. It's inconsistent with the god I've created in my head.* But a strong man accepts truths that make him wince. He embraces moral absolutes, teachings that exclude and offend, and doctrines that are out of step with modern public opinion.

Jesus had the courage to counter the wisdom of his day. Do you?

TRAIL MARKER 4: DISCERNING YOUR MISSION AND PUTTING ASIDE DISTRACTIONS

Jesus had a personal mission. He knew what he had to accomplish during his brief visit to our planet. He mentioned the mission several times during his journey of strength. Here's the first mission briefing, recorded in Matthew 16:

From that time on Jesus began to explain to his disciples that he must go to Jerusalem and suffer many things at the hands of the elders, chief priests and teachers of the law, and that he must be killed and on the third day be raised to life. (v. 21)

Here's what happened next:

Peter took him aside and began to rebuke him. "Never, Lord!" he said. "This shall never happen to you!"

Jesus turned and said to Peter, "Get behind me, Satan! You are a stumbling block to me; you do not have in mind the things of God, but the things of men." (vv. 22–23)

As soon as you discern your mission in life, a distraction will pop up. For Jesus, it was a know-it-all disciple. So what's your distraction?

There's an old saying: "If the devil can't make you bad, he'll make you busy." God has a mission for your life, but if the enemy can keep you distracted, you'll never fulfill your destiny. You'll fail to accomplish the task for which you were born. You'll spend your strength on things that don't matter and miss a chance to invest your life in something that will never pass away.

Many people live distracted lives. Work is demanding. Bills must be paid. Kids are overscheduled. Hobbies abound, and opportunities beckon. And I haven't even mentioned church—perhaps the biggest distraction of all. Church is the ideal place to hide from your mission. Congregations offer a shopping mall of volunteer opportunities—in exchange for your time. While some of these activities bear real fruit, others are just sanctified distractions that keep us from "forcefully advancing" God's kingdom. You can sing in the church choir for thirty years and completely miss the adventure God has for you.

I encourage you to look at the items in your schedule and ask yourself, *Is this really making a difference?* Examine your church activities and ask, *Is this advancing the mission God has given me?* If you don't know what your mission is, ask God for one. Every day. Bug him. You only get one life. Don't waste it doing things that don't matter.

TRAIL MARKER 5: PLACING GOD BEFORE FAMILY

Jesus made incredible demands on would-be disciples. He didn't just call people to follow him—he told them to abandon their money (Matthew 19:21), their homes (8:20), and even their loved ones (10:37). With Jesus, it was all or nothing. And it was now or never.

In modern Christianity, we give lip service to this. We teach publicly that God must have first place. But in reality, there is one thing that comes before Christ—family time. Churchgoing men have learned that they can use family activities as a get-out-of-God-free card. All a man has to say is, "Sorry, I can't come to the men's retreat. My son's got a hockey game," and he's given a pass.

Yet Jesus clearly and repeatedly elevated discipleship above family attachments during his journey of strength:

- "Anyone who loves his father or mother more than me is not worthy of me; anyone who loves his son or daughter more than me is not worthy of me" (10:37).

- "Someone told him [Jesus], 'Your mother and brothers are standing outside, wanting to speak to you.' He replied to him, 'Who is my mother, and who are my brothers?' Pointing to his disciples, he said, 'Here are my mother and my brothers. For whoever does the will of my Father in heaven is my brother and sister and mother'" (12:47–50).
- "Another disciple said to him, 'Lord, first let me go and bury my father.' But Jesus told him, 'Follow me, and let the dead bury their own dead'" (8:21–22).

Wow. That's harsh. Imagine getting a phone call like this:

VOICE ON PHONE. Hi, this is Kenny from the church. I'm calling to invite you to the men's breakfast Saturday morning.

YOU. Sorry, Kenny. My mom died and the funeral is Saturday.

KENNY. Let the old crone bury herself. You be at that breakfast!

Okay, that's a pretty ridiculous example. But it underscores the priority Jesus put on discipleship. First-century Jewish society was family oriented to the extreme—so Jesus' repeated demands for first place would have generated no little controversy.

I know fathers who boast, "I've never missed one of my son's games." Congratulations. It's a good thing to attend your kids' extracurricular activities. But if you are neglecting your spiritual life to be at every soccer match, then you and your kids will pay down the road. Think of the message you're sending to your children:

1. Your kids are the center of the universe.
2. Your pursuits are more important than God.
3. Spiritual development comes somewhere down the priority list.

As your children hurtle toward adolescence, is this what you want them to believe about themselves? About God?

Men, it's okay to tell your son you're going to miss one of his games because you're attending the men's retreat at church. In fact, I'd say it's very healthy to do this now and then. It teaches the boy that he is important, but that life is not all about him. It illustrates the importance you attach to your walk with Christ (a message he will absorb from your example). And when you come home from the retreat full of God's Spirit, your son will notice.

A word of caution before we move on: don't go to the other extreme. Some men become so involved at church that they neglect their families. I've known men who've used their commitment to Christ as an excuse to emotionally abandon their loved ones. That's a no-no as well. Jesus didn't ignore or abuse his family; he merely gave it proper place.

TRAIL MARKER 6: INVITING CONFLICT AS THE WAY TO PEACE

Curious thing about Jesus—the man who said "Blessed are the peacemakers" seemed to revel in conflict. Remember that famous proverb: "A gentle answer turns away wrath" (Proverbs 15:1)? Well, Christ seems to have scratched that one out of his Bible—at least during his second journey. Whenever Jesus saw a spark, he threw gasoline on it.

One such instance saw Jesus invited to a dinner party

at the home of a Pharisee (Luke 11:37–54). The host asked Christ a simple question: why don't you wash your hands before eating? (Ceremonial washing was the custom among observant Jews in those days. Since Jesus advertised himself as a rabbi, this would have been expected.)

If I were Jesus, I probably would have answered, "First, let me thank you for inviting me to dinner. That lamb smells delicious. Now, I'll answer your good question with one of my own: which is more important—to clean the inside of the cup, or the outside?" Such a cordial reply would have led to an evening of good conversation and healthy debate.

But Jesus didn't even try to be nice. He not only bit the hand that fed him, he practically tore it off. "You Pharisees clean the outside of the cup and dish, but inside you are full of greed and wickedness," he roared. From there Christ amped up his rhetoric, ridiculing the Pharisees' legalism and self-importance. He then descended to name-calling, labeling his hosts "unmarked graves." He concluded his diatribe by blaming their forefathers for murdering the prophets and apostles.

Whew. Doesn't this seem to be a bit of an overreaction to an honest question about religious hygiene? And this is how Jesus treated someone who had invited him to dinner! I can't remember the last party I attended at which a guest leveled murder charges against his hosts and their ancestors.

So I challenge you to answer this question: If we are supposed to be imitators of Christ, how on earth are we supposed to imitate *this*? Is Jesus giving us a green light to blast our opponents? To call people names? To nurse ancient grudges?

Well, no. There is a positive takeaway from the Lord's outburst. Believe it or not, Jesus is demonstrating the art of peacemaking. Really. Christ's volcanic reaction is an extreme example of how real peacemaking begins. In this dustup with the Pharisees, Christ was illustrating the first step of true peacemaking: bold truth-telling. These Pharisees had been lied to their entire lives. Their traditions told them they were made holy by their pious rituals. So Jesus' savage rebuke was an act of love. He was chopping away at the religious thicket that imprisoned the hearts of these children of God, wielding the sharp machete of truth. That's courageous peacemaking.

Most Christians are not very good at peacemaking, but we're experts at peace*keeping*. There is a difference. Whereas a peacemaker boldly seeks a long-term, sustainable peace between warring factions, a peacekeeper simply places a bandage over wounds and pretends they're not there. This happens in church all the time. A conflict breaks out between two families. Instead of dealing with it directly and decisively (as Jesus instructs us in Matthew 18), we pacify. We pretend everything is okay. The warring parties smile and grit their teeth on Sunday morning, but the rest of the week they engage in gossip and backstabbing. Eventually the church may even split—because peacekeeping is no substitute for peacemaking.

The same thing happens when church denominations debate controversial issues. Instead of practicing definitive peacemaking (fight it out, declare a winner, and move on), denominational leaders paper over the conflicts in the name of "unity and peace." But the underlying wounds continue to fester. Every year they pop up at the general assembly meeting. The press goes wild. Churches are torn apart. How much better if these organizations had years ago followed Jesus' example by embracing conflict rather than avoiding it?

In your personal life, are you a peacemaker or a peacekeeper? When you're facing a tough conversation, do you avoid it? When you are at odds with someone else, do you seek immediate resolution or steer clear? A man who would walk in strength must not skirt conflict but rather wade into it, seeing it as a growth opportunity for everyone. Just tell the truth. This is the essence of strength.

———————

My wife disciples women, many of whom are married to mean-spirited, grouchy men. She grimaced as she read this chapter. "David, I know men who will read this and see it as a green light to torment their wives and kids." I see the potential danger as well.

So, men, here is your official warning: the journey of strength is not a heavenly license to harass people. It is not permission to be as nasty as you wanna be.

You must never forget: the foundation of strength is submission and the attitude of humility that goes with it. If you abandon the lessons of submission as you practice strength, your foundation will crack. The house will come down. God's strength always grows from a root of grace, gentleness, and love.

———————

As I observe men in the church today, the great problem is not that they're too strong, bold, and aggressive. No, the vast majority of Christian men are too gentle, meek, and passive. Somehow they've missed discipleship's first major turn. They see the whole Christian journey as leading in the direction of submission. And no one is telling them any different.

Men, don't miss discipleship's first turn. And if you follow Jesus into a journey of strength, he may take you places that feel a bit ungodly. That's because, psychologically, you're going back in the masculine direction you were headed when you were running from God. Subconsciously, this may feel like sin. But it is not—as long as your house remains fixed to the rock of submission.

Chapter 15

THE JOURNEY
OF SACRIFICE

Mountaineers tell me the upper reaches of a peak are often the most difficult. You feel as though you're inside a Ping-Pong ball, with no horizon—not a single rock, tree, or other marker to tell you which way is up. Relentless winds drive the cold to your skin, no matter how many layers you're wearing. You walk a knife's edge as ridges converge and steepen. There's the discouragement of false summits, dwindling provisions, and malfunctioning equipment. Frustration mounts as you may spend days hunkered down in a tent, waiting out a storm. Routine tasks like cooking, sanitation, and even breathing become monumental undertakings in the punishing cold. Many climbers can't handle the strain. They abandon their quests and return to the relative comfort of base camp.

The final stage of a mountain climb offers many parallels to the journey of sacrifice. It's the hardest of the three. Very few men attempt it. As you move up the mountain, your climbing partners are likely to abandon you. Tasks that were once easy are now blindingly difficult. Black and white fade to endless gray. You can't shake the feeling you may have made a wrong turn somewhere. You discover you're standing on a false summit.

Jesus faced challenges like these during his journey of sacrifice. He was abandoned. Betrayed. His grief and sorrow became almost unbearable. His body absorbed inhuman punishment. He was given an impossible task: carry a heavy wooden cross after a severe beating. He was falsely accused, wrongly convicted, tortured, pierced, and murdered.

I pray that your third journey is not as difficult as Christ's. But it may be. As his disciple, you must be prepared to give your life for Jesus at any time. This year alone more than one hundred thousand men and women around the world will be tortured and killed for their faith in Christ.

But the third journey is not a death cult. Although some pay the ultimate price for their faith, the journey of sacrifice is not about dying. It never has been. The journey of sacrifice is really about *defeating* death by extending your life and influence beyond your time here on earth. This is why Jesus allowed himself to be sacrificed—so he could live on in the hearts of those who invite him to enter there.

As I speak to men, many have a hard time seeing the journey of sacrifice as *feminine*. Guys tell me, "David, sacrifice isn't feminine. It's the manliest thing a guy can do." I agree. Sacrifice is the pinnacle of manhood.

But the way of sacrifice requires you to do things that, on

their face, can seem unmanly. Sacrifice requires you to once again embrace weakness, dependency, and relationships. You relinquish your power and entrust it to others. As you walk the final journey, God knocks off the last of your hard edges. Rigidity and judgmentalism pass away. Legalism drowns in a torrent of God's love and grace. The third journey isn't a sprint to the feminine side of the mountain; it's more upward than leftward.

I'm having a hard time writing this chapter, because my journey of sacrifice has barely begun. I'm in my forties, and it has been less than a decade since I began walking in strength. But the Lord has begun whispering to me about this journey. The kids are growing up. Marriage is a comfortable fit. So I'm wondering, how can I invest the second half of my life for the greatest return? I don't know what God has for me, but he is already asking me to embrace a deeper weakness, humility, and dependence on him.

Look again at Gerasimos's metaphors for the journey of sacrifice:

- *Driving the direction you don't want to go.* The disciple makes his final journey in the feminine direction, as he is stripped of the strength he acquired during his second.
- *Sending the horse to stud.* Sacrifice is about reproduction—duplicating yourself in the next generation of men.
- *The roof of the building.* Your life becomes a layer of protection that covers those entrusted to you. You absorb the punishing wind, rain, hail, and snow so that those under your care don't have to.

- *New York to Mount Athos.* As you climb the mountain, fewer and fewer men will join you. That's why it's essential to keep climbing partners in sight.
- *The tree's final disposition.* The same Jesus who grew you into a mighty tree will now cut you down and engineer you into the object he chooses.

Let's spend a moment on that last one. Imagine a master woodworker walking through a forest. He fells a tree. Examining the timber's density and grain, the craftsman knows instantly the best use of this specimen. Certain lumber is not suitable to be worked and is split for firewood. But other wood shows potential. After a period of seasoning, the woodworker shapes it into whatever he chooses: a chair, a guitar neck, a plank, or a broom handle. The tree, which was destined to die anyway, now has a chance to "live on"—years, decades, or even centuries beyond its normal life span—as something useful to the master who repurposed it.

Sacrifice is about allowing God to cut you down and make you into the object he chooses. If you walk the third journey, you have the opportunity to live forever—not just in heaven, but here on earth, through your legacy. The reason you are a Christian today is because somewhere in history, a man just like you walked the journey of sacrifice. He poured out his life for Jesus, and through his legacy, you are reaping the benefits. Although you will never know his name, you are standing on this dead man's shoulders. In a sense, he is living through you.

Before we examine the trail markers of the journey of sacrifice, here are a few observations about your third and final journey.

THE JOURNEY OF SACRIFICE
IS SHORT

Although Jesus begins preparing for this journey midway through the gospel of Matthew, the journey itself consumes less than a week of his life. In terms of word count, it represents just one-seventh of the gospel of Matthew. (In contrast, John devotes the final 40 percent of his gospel to the journey of sacrifice. This is not surprising, since John writes from a more feminine, relational perspective than the other three gospel writers.)

THE JOURNEY OF SACRIFICE
IS LINKED WITH OLD AGE

The journey of sacrifice is reflected in the physical process of aging. As a man gets old, nature strips away his physical strength. He must swallow his pride and let others help him. In exchange, he accrues wisdom and experience. Some men seize this opportunity to become givers; others focus on their decline and become takers.

THE THIRD JOURNEY CLOSELY
MIRRORS THE FIRST

During your journey of sacrifice, you will once again learn the lessons you did in the journey of submission, but at a much higher level.

Ready to reach for the summit? Here we go.

TRAIL MARKER 1: FOCUSING ON SACRIFICE

Sacrifice wasn't something that just happened to Christ. His arrest, trial, and crucifixion weren't a run of bad luck. Jesus saw the oncoming train and threw himself down on the tracks. Christ looked past the suffering and pain and kept his eyes fixed on the endgame.

In the same way, we men will have the greatest impact on this earth as we focus on the endgame. Like Jesus, we must look forward to the day our powers are taken. This is something I struggle with. Like most men, I fear losing control. My nightmare is to become incapacitated and dependent on others.

As old age and physical limitations engulf me, is it possible I can still be a spiritual powerhouse? I've known such men. Flat on their backs, hardly able to move, these men crackled with the Spirit's power.

Men, dark days will eventually come. Ask God, *How do I go out on top? What steps can I take today to make my eventual sacrifice worthy of you?*

TRAIL MARKER 2: EXPECTING BETRAYAL WITHOUT FREAKING OUT ABOUT IT

Jesus knew he was going to be betrayed. He even told his buddies it was going to happen—and that one of them would be his betrayer.

Know this: if Christ was betrayed, you will be too. Jesus

told his disciples it would happen to them (see Matthew 10:17–22). The apostle Paul was abandoned and betrayed by several men he personally mentored (2 Timothy 4:10). Joseph was sold into slavery by his own brothers (Genesis 37:28).

Unfortunately, a lot of men are wimps. They think they've got the right to quit the church and turn their backs on God when they're treated poorly. "Oh, I've quit going to church because the people weren't very friendly," they moan. "My pastor turned out to be a hypocrite, so I dropped out." Or they stretch, "What about the famous televangelist who went to jail? It's his fault I left the church."

Guys, buck up. Don't quit your faith because someone you admired let you down. Instead, consider yourself blessed. God has chosen you worthy to experience a small fraction of the betrayal that Jesus himself faced.

You will be betrayed by a fellow Christian. Expect it. Rejoice in it.

TRAIL MARKER 3: WAIVING THE RIGHT TO ACT ON YOUR OWN BEHALF

Whenever I read the story of Christ's arrest and trial, a voice inside my heart says, *C'mon, Jesus. Don't be a wimp—speak up! Defend yourself already*. For years I was puzzled that Christ stood silent as false charges rained down.

Jesus had unlimited power at his disposal. He could have taken control of the situation with the blink of an eye. He said so: "Do you think that I cannot appeal to my Father, and he will at once send me more than twelve legions of angels?" (Matthew 26:53 ESV).

Yet Christ chose to not use his power. Why? We all know

the Sunday school answer: Jesus had to die to redeem human-kind. But there's another lesson for men who would walk the third journey.

In the first journey we learn to depend on God, but our third journey demands a deeper dependence. I call it "holy passivity." We learn to pray and then to allow God to act on our behalf, even when we have the ability to take matters into our own hands.

Remember Frodo, the heroic hobbit in the Lord of the Rings trilogy? He possessed a magic ring of power. Whenever he put the ring on his finger, he became invisible to his ene-mies. But in doing so, he made his location known to the evil Sauron. Human power always comes at a price.

TRAIL MARKER 4: GIVING UP YOUR RIGHT TO A HAPPY ENDING

Jesus could have skipped his journey of sacrifice. He could have started a megasynagogue and become the best-known rabbi in the Middle East, dispensing God's Word to crowds hungry for the truth. Jesus accomplished so much in just three years of ministry; imagine what he could have done in forty! After a long, successful preaching career, Christ could have handed the synagogue to Peter and retired to a little cottage on the shores of Galilee.

A lot of folks look forward to a comfortable retirement of sunshine, fishing, golf, and Botox. Hear me: none of these things is a sin. It's not wrong to plan for the future or to enjoy a relaxing retirement. But when a happy ending becomes our primary focus, then we're in danger of missing the final journey.

The Bible says, "Is not wisdom found among the aged?

Does not long life bring understanding?" (Job 12:12). Our churches are full of old men. Maybe you're one of them. Now that you understand the three journeys, ask God for an opportunity to go back down the mountain and share some of that wisdom and understanding with the younger climbers. Never be afraid to trade a little bit of comfort for a lot of joy.

TRAIL MARKER 5: MOVING MORE DEEPLY INTO THE FEMININE

I read a lot of Christian books written by older men. God has given great wisdom to men like Tony Campolo, Leonard Sweet, and Eugene Peterson. But I've noticed something about these men: the older they get, the more feminine their musings become. Their theology gets softer and more pliable. I think I know why.

As these lions of the faith grow old, they hear God calling them back to the feminine side of the mountain. Larry Crabb is a prolific Christian writer in his sixties. His most recent book is titled *Sixty-Six Love Letters*. It's built on the premise that God is a betrayed lover wooing us back into his arms so we can enjoy the love of family forever.[1]

God as my lover? Christianity as a holy romance? Yuck. Such metaphors don't really turn my crank. But musings like these are a reflection of Jesus calling these third-journey climbers back to the sacred feminine.

Have you noticed that old guys who have walked closely with God often become mystics? These men turn up their well-educated noses at easy answers, black-and-white decision–making, and formulaic Christianity. If I may use another awkward metaphor, many of these aged saints seem to have *fallen in love with Jesus Christ*. Now you know why: the Lord's final call requires a feminine response.

Of course, the great danger of this journey is the temptation to leave biblical authority behind—to see life exclusively through the prism of love and to jettison the law. A surprising number of men (especially well-educated ones) follow the feminine call right over a cliff. They forget the lessons of their first two journeys and, without realizing it, begin following a comforting god of their own making. (More about this in our next chapter, under Danger Point 6.)

TRAIL MARKER 6: ENTRUSTING YOUR WORK TO THE NEXT GENERATION

Imagine this conversation in heaven, just before Christ was born:

ANGEL. So, Jesus, what's your plan?
JESUS. I'm going to earth, where I'll train a dozen common men. After three years, I'll leave it to them to change the world.
ANGEL. That seems kind of risky. What's your plan B?
JESUS. There is no plan B.

Jesus placed the fate of the world in the hands of twelve ordinary men. He designated them his chosen successors, trained them thoroughly, and set them loose to continue his work. Yes, they had the Holy Spirit to help them, but that's still a lot of trust to place in twelve also-rans.

If only our high-profile Christian leaders understood this. These men get addicted to power, and they don't relinquish it happily. How many times have we seen a church or parachurch ministry implode after the death of its founder? Or worse, the old man designates a successor, but then refuses to let go. As I write this, one of America's most famous television preachers has just fired his protégé (his own son) and has taken back control of the ministry. Donations, viewership, and attendance are way down.

The transition from strength to sacrifice is excruciating for high-powered men. We get used to being in charge. We know the system better than anyone—after all, we built it. And we love the perks. Our self-image gets tied up in our work.

But the third-journey disciple is always trying to work himself out of a job. Any man who wants his legacy to proceed beyond his death will actively seek and groom his successor (or successors).

You may not be a high-profile preacher. But as you walk in strength, God will give you something to do. It's never too early to start looking for an individual who will carry on the work after you are gone. Reproduction is the heart of sacrifice.

TRAIL MARKER 7: MAKING A FINAL SURRENDER TO WHATEVER LIFE BRINGS

Every man will meet death one day. And as you age, scary things will happen to you. Things involving needles. Wheelchairs. Catheters.

Don't be surprised when suffering comes (1 Peter 4:12). When the Bible tells us to rejoice in suffering (Romans 5:3), it's not just talking about being imprisoned for our faith. We must be strong whatever comes our way. When

I'm eighty-nine, I hope I'm still investing in younger men, instead of focusing on my aches and pains. Perhaps I'll be able to say what Jesus did as he faced death: "Nevertheless not my will, but thine, be done" (Luke 22:42 KJV).

Chapter 16

WHERE MEN GET LOST ON THE MOUNTAIN

There are many ways to die on a mountain.

You can drop into a crevasse. You can fall over the edge. A rope can fail. You can be buried in an avalanche. Some climbers die of hypoxia or "mountain sickness." Others freeze to death. I just read the story of a well-respected physician who perished on the slopes of Mount Hood when a rock broke loose from a snowy overhang and crashed into his body, sending him tumbling a thousand feet to his death.

Or you can just get lost.

Every year, millions of men give their lives to Christ. But many fade away as they journey up the mountain. Very few reach the pinnacle of manhood. In this chapter, we examine seven Danger Points where men tend to lose the trail.

DANGER POINT 1: GETTING STUCK
AT BASE CAMP

The church is a vast spiritual base camp, home to millions of men who have started their journey with Christ but have never moved up the mountain.

Base camp is home to men like Religious Rick. He grew up in church. He knows the rituals. He attends church regularly, prays occasionally, and crosses himself before each meal. But he's not truly walking with Christ. He dismisses men who are more committed than he is—labeling them "religious fanatics."

Base camp is also home to Saved Sammy. Many years ago Sammy made a one-time decision to "invite Jesus into his heart." Today Sammy describes himself as spiritual but not religious. He believes in God and claims to follow Jesus, but his faith makes little impact on his daily life.

Then there's Pretender Pete. He goes to church, but he's stuck in the manly foothills. He hasn't even begun a walk with Christ. (A lot of Pretender Petes are dragged to church by their wives, girlfriends, and mothers.)

You probably know men like Rick, Sammy, and Pete who are loitering around the base of the mountain. How do we get more of these men out of the foothills and on to their ascent? There is a way, and we'll discuss it in chapter 19.

DANGER POINT 2: SKIPPING SUBMISSION
AND GOING STRAIGHT TO STRENGTH

Remember Samson? His ham-fisted efforts to serve God in his own strength created a blast zone of death, destruction, and suffering. In the New Testament, the Pharisees also tried this route. These religious know-it-alls memorized 613 laws, yet they somehow missed the two greatest commandments: *Love God* and *Love your neighbor*.

Pastors sometimes fall into the strength trap—particularly talented, magnetic preachers who can draw a crowd with their personal charisma. I know of a church that recently fired its longtime minister. "Pastor Gil" could preach the paint off the walls. A gifted evangelist, Gil could step into the pulpit and sneeze, and dozens would give their lives to Jesus. But somehow, Gil had skipped the journey of submission (or more likely, forgotten its lessons as his strength increased). As it turns out, Pastor Gil was a control freak. He verbally abused his staff. Gil used his power to intimidate and bully others. He misled his congregation.

I would guess that fewer than 5 percent of churchgoing men make this error. But these men leave a tornado path of ruin in their wake. This is why it is so important for proud men to be humbled. However, an excessive focus on humility leads to a far more prevalent problem, which is our next danger point.

DANGER POINT 3: GETTING STUCK ON THE FEMININE FLANK OF THE MOUNTAIN

Here we find men who are humble, meek, and absolutely useless to God's kingdom. The left flank is the domain of the passive Christian Nice Guy. He's a man who has followed the journey of submission to its logical conclusion: Since Jesus is so tender, loving, gentle, and kind, I also must be tender, loving, gentle, and kind. All the time. Any other response is un-Christian.

One time I was attending a large gathering of men's ministry leaders. Our keynote speaker was a veteran pastor. We'll call him Matt. His topic: "How to Be a Servant Leader."

Pastor Matt was a Christian Nice Guy with a revealing story to tell. "The woman's name was Rhoda," he said. "She was a founding member of the church, but she was no Christian. Rhoda was mean, hateful, and petty—a gossip who stirred up opposition to everything I tried to accomplish. Rhoda came to my office at least once a month to tell me all the ways I was failing as a preacher.

"Eventually, I came to despise Rhoda," he continued. "I've gotta be honest—there were times I wanted to punch Rhoda in the nose. But whenever I saw her, I would ask myself, *What would Jesus do?* And I would see a vision of our Lord taking up a towel and washing this woman's feet. So for years I served her humbly. I absorbed her blows. I let her backbiting and gossiping roll off my back. Eventually, she destroyed the church. Split it right in two, but I never spoke a harsh word to her. Instead, I loved her, because that's what Jesus would have done."

I couldn't believe what I was hearing. In front of two hundred men, here stood a pastor boasting of how he'd allowed a selfish, bitter woman to emasculate him and destroy his congregation. *That's what Jesus would have done?* I think even journey-of-submission Jesus would have picked up a whip and driven this Jezebel out of the church!

As Pastor Matt wrapped up his story, I looked around the roomful of men's ministry leaders. I expected them to be as appalled as I was, but instead I saw heads nodding in agreement. There was a clear consensus among these men: Matt had done exactly as Jesus would have done. He had turned the other cheek (Matthew 5:39). He had loved an enemy (Matthew 5:44). He had modeled the fruit of the

Spirit (Galatians 5:22–23). And even though his church was left a smoldering ruin, God had been glorified.

Like all good Christian men, Pastor Matt began his spiritual journey by moving in the feminine direction. But he made a fatal assumption along the way: *God wants me to move in this direction my entire life. If I'm to be like Jesus, I must become ever softer, ever weaker, and ever gentler. When bad things happen, I must absorb the blows and suffer quietly, just as the Lord did.*

Incredibly, after growing up in Sunday school, attending seminary, and preaching for thirty-five years, Pastor Matt managed to misplace the Jesus of Matthew 8–25. Somewhere along the line, Matt began serving a half-Jesus based on the first and third journeys. Following this half-Jesus caused him to devolve into a door-Matt, because that's what you become when you focus solely on the feminine side of the mountain.

DANGER POINT 4: REFUSING THE JOURNEY OF STRENGTH

I've noticed a pattern in the Bible:

1. God speaks to a man (or sends a messenger to speak for him).
2. The man is given an assignment.
3. The man questions his orders.
4. God goes to extreme lengths to get his attention.

Moses, Gideon, Balaam, Jonah, Zechariah—some of Scripture's marquee names initially refused their journeys of strength.

I'm convinced that God still calls men to great deeds.

But like the heroes of old, modern men offer excuses. I don't think this is due to rebelliousness or reluctance. It's surprise.

> INNER VOICE. Hello, Ernie? It's God.
>
> ERNIE. Yes, Lord?
>
> INNER VOICE. Ernie, you've done a nice job submitting to me. Your heart is soft. You're being very loving. Well done.
>
> ERNIE. Why, thank you, Lord.
>
> INNER VOICE. Son, it's time for you to get in touch with your masculine side again. Start taking some risks. Get aggressive. Stop being so nice.
>
> ERNIE. But, Lord, that's the direction I was headed when I was a hell-bound idiot. [*Pause.*] Lord, is that really you?

If you are walking in submission, the day will come when God calls you to strength. And it will feel wrong to you. Frightening. Maybe even sinful. You'll probably resist, just as the patriarchs did. I hope God doesn't have to speak through a burning bush, a gulping whale, or a chatty ass to get your attention.

DANGER POINT 5: CAMPING ON THE MASCULINE FLANK

We've all heard stories of churchmen who've become drunk with power. Some men use the church to gain control over others. Others see their congregation as a personal harem—a place to meet people for sex. Charlatans wrap their get-rich-quick schemes in religious lingo, to more easily fleece the faithful. I just read about a prosperity-gospel preacher in an impoverished nation who owns nine homes, a fleet of SUVs, and a private jet. He wears five-thousand-dollar suits and never travels without a quartet of bodyguards.

I've seen religiously proud men who wield God's Word like a club, using it not to bless but to oppress. They throw themselves into the Scriptures, sculpting a perfect doctrine. But when life throws a curve, their rigid theology cracks. Daughter gets pregnant? Cover it up to save the family's reputation at the church. Shuttle her off for a quiet abortion. Or publicly shame her for promiscuity and reject her in front of friends and family. Such men are doctrinally correct but bereft of love.

How do we avoid getting stuck on the masculine flank? The answer is found in one of my favorite passages, 1 Corinthians 16:13: "Be on your guard; stand firm in the faith; be men of courage; be strong." Boo-yah! It doesn't get much more masculine than that. But look at the next verse: "Do everything in love." That's the key, men. We must keep our feet planted on the bedrock of submission even as we learn to wield heaven's strength. A submissive, humble, loving heart will keep us from overdosing on power.

DANGER POINT 6: TRYING TO CLIMB THE FEMININE FLANK OF THE MOUNTAIN

Climbing the left flank is a treacherous route, upon which many a man loses his theological footing. Some plunge to their spiritual deaths, completely abandoning the faith.

When I was a senior in college, I was considering graduate work at a prestigious seminary. The school had been established in the 1800s as a training center for young pastors and missionaries. But a century later, the seminary's focus had completely changed. In fact, the faculty council had just signed a paper denouncing cross-cultural evangelism as a tool of Western imperialism. Many of the professors at this divinity school were openly agnostic or atheist.

How does this happen? Why do some Christians (particularly well-educated ones) abandon biblical orthodoxy even as they study the Scriptures? The answer may be as simple as this: these scholars follow feminine half-Jesus right off the left edge of the mountain.

Reason with me: if a man sees God completely in soft terms (benign, loving, accepting, merciful, etc.), then it's a short walk to misunderstandings like these:

Universalism. God is love, so how can he punish anyone? All religions ultimately lead us to the same loving God. Since everyone is going to heaven, evangelism becomes a pointless exercise in imposing our views on others.

Sin. Jesus loved and accepted everyone. Our job is to spread that extravagant welcome to others, regardless of their personal behavior. Our private moral choices don't matter that much.

Pacifism. Jesus told us to love our enemies, so war is never justified—even when we are attacked. Jesus told us, "Do not resist an evil person" (Matthew 5:39). How can we even maintain an army when Paul commanded, "Do not repay anyone evil for evil. . . . But overcome evil with good" (Romans 12:17, 21)?

There's more. When we focus all our attention on Jesus' feminine characteristics, we can come to distrust any behavior or attitude that seems masculine. For example:

A deep suspicion of guy things. I once met a Lutheran pastor who was ridiculed by his fellow seminarians for having grown up on a ranch. One of his classmates snarked, "A ranch? You've repented of that, haven't you?" I know of pastors who seem to distrust anything pertaining to men, including hunting and fishing, the military, action movies, law enforcement, sports, high-performance cars, firearms, and so forth. This suspicion also affects our view of acceptable Christian behavior. Example: Most churches would happily sponsor a Ladies' Scrapbooking Night, but most would quickly oppose a Men's Cigar Night. Neither scrapbooking nor smoking is mentioned in the Bible, but the male-oriented activity instinctively raises our hackles. In the church, we tend to see guy things as sinful, silly, or sophomoric.

Distrust of certainty. The very idea that our religion is right while others might be wrong is deeply offensive to men who live on the feminine flank. Gene Robinson, the Episcopal Church's first gay bishop, is a prime advocate of this line of thinking. Invited to pray at the inauguration of President Barack Obama, Robinson studied past inaugural prayers and was "horrified" at how "specifically and aggressively Christian they were." Robinson promised, "This will not be a Christian prayer, and I won't be quoting Scripture or anything like that." In the end, Robinson, an ordained minister of the gospel, addressed his prayer not to Jesus, but rather to the "God of Our Many Understandings."[1] Robinson's feminized theology abhors the masculine traits of certainty and exclusivity.

Excessive self-examination, bordering on self-hatred. I've noticed that women will often pick at themselves. Watch a woman as she walks past a mirror—she'll frown, thinking she's too fat, or her clothes don't match, or her makeup is smudged. Women buy most of the self-help books because they sense there's something wrong with them. A similar self-loathing afflicts men who walk the feminine flank. In an effort to be humble, they lapse into a mind-set that says, "We're always wrong, while others are always right." These men feel we're far more Christian when we judge ourselves harshly, blame ourselves first, and feel bad for our blessings. Instead of being grateful for what they have, they walk around in a fog of guilt because they aren't suffering enough. Of course, individual Bible passages can be twisted to justify this pernicious theology.

DANGER POINT 7: SKIPPING THE FIRST TWO JOURNEYS AND MOVING STRAIGHT TO SACRIFICE

On Good Friday, Ruben Enaje was arrested and dragged through the streets of his village by men posing as soldiers. A crown of thorns was placed on his head. Blood flowed down his face as his captors stretched him out on a cross and drove seven-inch nails into his hands and feet. Enaje was hoisted upright as crowds of tourists and neighbors looked on. After a few minutes he was taken down and another penitent was nailed in his place. This was the twenty-second time Ruben Enaje had been crucified.

Some men identify so strongly with Christ's final journey that they try to join him in sacrifice right away. In the Philippines, men like Ruben Enaje endure public crucifixion each Easter as penance for their sins. Hundreds of other Filipinos practice self-flagellation—stripping to the waist and whipping themselves with chains until their backs are a bloody mess.

These practices—along with asceticism and some forms of monasticism—arise when we focus too much on the journey of sacrifice. Self-denial is a necessary component of the Christian life, but it is not an end in itself. Nor is it meant to become the focus of our life on earth. As we learned in the previous chapter, sacrifice is meant to be the final act in the life of a disciple—not the entire journey. The Bible is clear: there is no benefit in suffering for suffering's sake. Its purpose is to build perseverance, character, and hope (Romans 5:3–4).

Men, your journey of sacrifice will come soon enough. A life devoted to harsh penance, ascetic self-denial, or monastic isolation is a life wasted.

―――――――――

When you were little, your parents told you to stay away from the edges of dangerous things. The street, the bridge, the swimming pool—these are places where you can get hurt if you're not careful.

In that spirit, I would add this word of caution: Beware of either flank of the mountain. This is where religious extremism hangs out.

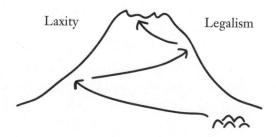

A graceless legalism occupies the airspace off the masculine side of the mountain. Meanwhile, a limp laxity inhabits the space off the feminine side. Men fall off these edges from time to time, but not you—because you have the map.

Men, stay focused on your goal—the summit. Work with God as he develops both sides of your character. Stay away from the edges. And never, never forget the lessons of one journey as you tackle the next.

Chapter 17

THE MAP:
A THOUSAND
AND ONE USES

I became the proud owner of a Swiss army knife on my eleventh birthday. This baby was loaded: two blades, scissors, punch, screwdriver tips, nail file, bottle opener, corkscrew (so useful to an eleven-year-old), and, of course, the little slide-in toothpick and tweezers. Half the fun was thinking up new uses for that pocket-sized tool.

Think of the three journeys of Jesus as a Swiss army knife for your spiritual life. As you begin walking the journeys, you'll find they have dozens of uses. The journeys are a tool you'll pull out and use frequently—for the rest of your life.

Here are a dozen "tools" you'll discover as you wrestle with the journeys. There are probably many more, but these twelve will get you started.

TOOL 1: THE THREE JOURNEYS ARE KEY TO BECOMING A GIANT OF A MAN

I'm going to make a bold statement: Every truly great man who has ever graced our world has walked some version of these three paths—regardless of whether that man was religious or not. Go ahead; read the biographies of history's giants. They often start life as untamed colts—strong but unruly. However, at some point these men undergo a period of humility and submission, followed by a rise to strength and often a final act of sacrifice on behalf of others.

Meanwhile, if you study the biographies of evil men who inflicted great pain on the world, you'll find a twisted path or a total abandonment of the three journeys, often stemming from a father who was absent or abusive.

You may never have desired to become a giant among men—but why not? Follow the path that leads to life, and you can achieve more than you ever thought possible.

TOOL 2: THE JOURNEYS EXPLAIN A LOT ABOUT LIFE AND THE NATURAL WORLD

The path to success in education, business, or politics often involves the three journeys. A successful marriage can also be seen as fitting the pattern.

Take the military as another example. A soldier's life begins with submission: eight weeks of basic training. Then the focus shifts toward specific training, which is a mixture of submission and strength. Eventually the soldier sees combat, where strength is tested. Sacrifice may involve pouring out one's life on the battlefield or, if the soldier survives, becoming a trainer of younger troops.

Open your eyes! You'll see the three journeys everywhere you look.

TOOL 3: THE JOURNEYS GIVE US A FILING SYSTEM FOR TRUTHS WE LEARN

We laugh at the perpetual college student—that slacker who attends random classes, absorbing good information but never graduating. He has no major and no goal, other than "being in college."

Yet this is exactly how we teach in the church—randomly. A typical visit to church might include an adult class on evangelism, a devotion encouraging more prayer, a bulletin insert on serving, and a sermon on money. This is all great truth, but it comes at men in such a haphazard fashion. There's no course of study, no overarching goal, and no sense that this Bible buffet is leading anywhere.

I was first informed of this problem by a sharp young man named Cal. "I'm more interested in serving God than ever," he said. "But I'm getting bored with church. It's not the pastor's fault—his sermons are great and full of truth. But it's all kind of directionless. I don't feel like I'm on a track that's leading me to something big. Frankly, if I'm going to invest this kind of time and energy, I need to see a goal."

Just as a file cabinet lends structure to your paperwork, the journeys can lend structure to your spiritual experiences. For instance, if you hear a message about dependence on God, file that under *submission*. If the pastor preaches on evangelism, put that under *strength*. If you read a devotion that challenges you to pour out your life for others, drop that into the file marked *sacrifice*.

As you learn new truths from preachers, classes, books, and friends, start mentally filing them by journey. You might just see a pattern emerge as God leads you up the mountain.

TOOL 4: THE JOURNEYS SHOW US WHY WE UNDERGO TRIALS

A popular bumper sticker proclaims, "Stuff happens." (Well, *stuff* isn't the exact word used, but I couldn't get the real word past my editor.)

Anyway, when *stuff* happens to you, the three journeys can help make sense of it. If your car breaks down, or you get laid off, or tragedy strikes, you can rejoice. Instead of thinking, *These things happened to me because God is against me*, you'll know the truth. Trials, setbacks, and challenges are a sign that God is teaching you to submit to him, no matter which journey you may be on.

The lesson of horse breaking can help us understand. The colt doesn't know why he's stuck in a corral with a man on his back. He can't understand why there's a rope around his head or a bit stuck in his mouth. He's thinking, *The man hates me. He's trying to abuse me. Get me out of here!*

Most of us react like untamed colts when trials come our way. We think God is mad at us. We wonder if he knows how much pain we're in. We think, *I wish God would just get off my back*. But trials are not punishments from God. He is breaking us—preparing us for important work to come. The quicker we submit, the shorter our journey of submission will be.

Now let's close the loop:

- If trials are the lessons of submission . . .

- and the journey of submission moves you in the feminine direction . . .
- then how should you react to trials? Like a girl.

I'm serious. When trials come, get help from friends. Run toward community, not away from it. Weep. Talk about it. Most men try to handle their problems themselves. They try to be strong and independent. Idiots! They're running toward the masculine side of the mountain, even as God is leading them the opposite way. So be smart—work with the Lord instead of against him. Handle your trials like a chick. It works.

TOOL 5: THE THREE JOURNEYS SHOW US THE PATH JESUS EXPECTS US TO WALK

There's a snippet of bad theology floating around the church: *God has created a unique path for every believer.* I'm skeptical. This puts a lot of pressure on us to find this mystical path— and if we overlook it, we miss out on God's will. Bummer.

But nothing in Scripture suggests that God ordains individual paths of discipleship. To be sure, each follower has unique experiences, but Jesus spoke of one road that leads to life. So rejoice! You don't have to waste any more time trying to search out that special path that God made just for you. Instead, follow the trail Christ blazed for us—the three journeys.

TOOL 6: THE JOURNEYS HELP US SEE WHAT'S COMING

Humans have a tendency to do what they think is best at the moment, instead of what's beneficial in the long run. A study of credit card users found that borrowers would often choose a low "teaser" interest rate even though it would end up costing them more over the long term. However, when they were given a diagram comparing the total costs, they usually chose the less-expensive card.

Think of the map as a diagram for your personal life. Use it to track your development as a man and as a disciple. The map also helps you set goals by revealing what's over the horizon. Why not begin asking God to prepare you for the next journey? The map helps you work with God's natural order instead of against it.

TOOL 7: THE JOURNEYS HELP US MAKE BETTER DECISIONS

One morning a while back, the phone rang. It was my son. He was up in Alaska; I was in Texas. His car was sitting dead in the parking lot of a grocery store. Wouldn't start. He called to ask my advice.

I love that.

When he was a teenager, he thought I was a dummy. But the older he gets, the smarter I become. I love helping him think through his options and arrive at the best decision.

God wants to help you with your decisions too. The next time you have a decision to make, use the three journeys as a guide. Here's how:

First, submit the decision to God. Take fifteen seconds to ask him to help you make the right decision. Tell him, "God, I've got this decision to make. I stop now and submit it to you. I need your wisdom." Sometimes this is all you have to do. God will guide—but he's waiting for you to ask.

Before you decide, here's another submissive thing you can do: seek the advice of wise men. Proverbs 12:15 says, "The way of a fool is right in his own eyes, but a wise man listens to advice" (ESV).

One more idea: submit your decision to God's Word. Search the Scriptures and see what they have to say about your situation. Use a computer Bible study tool that lets you search by topic and keyword. A little bit of homework may save you from a bonehead decision.

Second, move forward in strength. Once you make your decision, advance in strength and confidence. Don't second-guess or look back. Act decisively. God gives strength to the bold.

I recently had an opportunity to make a move that would have helped my writing and speaking career. I prayed about it and felt confident. But for some reason I procrastinated. I decided to do a little more thinking. I vacillated. The opportunity passed, and now I'm suffering the consequences. Please learn from my mistake: once you make your decision, transition quickly into strength.

Third, review your decision through the lens of sacrifice. A bit of feminine introspection long after a decision is made can help you arrive at better decisions in the future. *What were the consequences of my decision? Did everyone benefit? How could I have made a better decision?* This is the *sacrifice* component of three-journeys decision-making.

This process isn't just for life-altering choices. Don't be afraid to use it with your routine, everyday calls. I'm never too busy to assist my kids, and God is always happy to help you. (By the way, my son got his car running that evening. He replaced the starter himself and saved about three hundred dollars.)

TOOL 8: THE JOURNEYS HELP US RESOLVE CONFLICT

When you are facing a disagreement, submission should be your first response. Be gentle. Preserve relationships. Don't fight back—be kind. Here's a well-known passage from Romans 12:

> If it is possible, as far as it depends on you, live at peace with everyone. Do not take revenge, my friends, but leave room for God's wrath, for it is written: "It is mine to avenge; I will repay," says the Lord. On the contrary: "If your enemy is hungry, feed him; if he is thirsty, give him something to drink. In doing this, you will heap burning coals on his head." Do not be overcome by evil, but overcome evil with good. (vv. 18–21)

Paul has given us good, solid first-journey advice. Successful conflict resolution always begins with a feminine response. Lavish kindness on your enemies.

I remember being taunted by a bully when I was young. Bruce was a sandy-haired loudmouth who always had an unkind word for me. My first instinct was to fight back and defend my pride. But my father gave me some great advice: "He's just trying to get a rise out of you. Next time he says something mean, agree with him. Just smile and say, 'Yes, Bruce, I'm a total loser. You're absolutely right.' Keep smiling and he'll lose interest." Sure enough, when I stopped letting Bruce get under my skin, he gave up. And best of all, my friends saw me not as a loser, but as a winner, because I had outfoxed my adversary.

But what do you do when a soft answer doesn't turn

away wrath? If submission doesn't work, you're permitted to move up to strength. Fight back. Defend yourself. Battle with words, and if it comes to blows, you're allowed to use force to resolve the conflict.

Here's another bully story: My son Tony spent his freshman year of high school on foreign exchange. He quickly ran afoul of a bully—a bantamweight who hated Tony because he was an American. On September 11, 2003, he brought a box-cutter knife to school and took a swipe at my son, saying he wished Tony had perished in the World Trade Center. The teachers turned a blind eye to the situation, so I advised Tony to defend himself vigorously. The next time his tormentor came around, Tony knocked him down and shoved his face into the dirt, forcing him to apologize—in English.

You probably can guess what happened: my son and his adversary eventually became best friends. Once you defeat the bully, it's important to be gracious and loving. Don't hold a grudge. It's time to be soft and feminine again.

See the journeys at work? Your first response to conflict is feminine. Try to work things out. If that fails, go masculine. Respond in strength. Once things are resolved, go feminine again. Matthew gave us the *Reader's Digest* version of three-journey conflict resolution in chapter 18 of his gospel. Jesus is speaking:

> If one of my followers sins against you, go and point out what was wrong. But do it in private, just between the two of you. If that person listens, you have won back a follower. But if that one refuses to listen, take along one or two others. The Scriptures teach that every complaint must be proven true by two or more witnesses. If the follower refuses to listen to them, report the matter to

the church. Anyone who refuses to listen to the church must be treated like an unbeliever or a tax collector. (vv. 15–17 CEV)

Our first response to conflict should be soft and conciliatory. If this fails, then it's okay to ramp up the testosterone. And you can take it up pretty high—all the way to expulsion from the church (Paul confirms this in Titus 3:10). However, if the miscreant genuinely repents anywhere along the way, we are to respond immediately with love and acceptance— forgiving seventy times seven (Matthew 18:21–22).

Initial response	Feminine: kind, compassionate
Secondary response	Masculine: progressively tougher
If he repents	Feminine: immediate love and acceptance

TOOL 9: THE JOURNEYS HELP US IN THE WORKPLACE

Correcting or disciplining wayward employees is one of the most difficult tasks facing a supervisor. Business gurus Kenneth Blanchard and Spencer Johnson, authors of *The One Minute Manager*, advise managers to use the "correction sandwich" approach.[1] First, offer the offender genuine words of praise, followed by words of correction, followed by words of encouragement. You start and end soft, putting the hard stuff in the middle.

Notice how closely this technique follows the pattern of the three journeys. Of course, you can use a correction sandwich when dealing with volunteers or family members as well.

TOOL 10: THE JOURNEYS
SHARPEN OUR TEACHING

Glenn has been leading a men's Bible study for years. Attendance always starts strong, but by the end of the semester, more than half the men drop out. Sound familiar?

Then Glenn learns about the three journeys. This time he decides to focus his teaching on the journey of strength. He announces that he's looking for "established disciples who want to strengthen their faith walk." He limits his group to men who have walked with Christ for five years or more.

Glenn grounds his teaching in Matthew 8–25. He brings in an object lesson each week. Guess what? His group no longer shrinks; it grows.

Once you understand the journeys, you can match your teaching to the audience you're trying to reach. If you're instructing a bunch of new Christians, focus on submission. Maturing believers should learn strength; and longtime saints should be taught sacrifice. Do this, and your students will rise up and call you blessed.

TOOL 11: THE JOURNEYS CAN BE
USED IN OUR WORSHIP SONGS

So many of today's praise and worship songs are reflections of the first journey. They focus on the softer side of our faith—love, grace, beauty, and mercy. The choruses are repetitive and simple—designed to stimulate the emotions rather than the mind. As a result, worship itself is becoming more feminine. (In my church, fewer than half the men actually sing the praise songs.)

If you're a composer, why not try a song that promotes

the second journey? It probably won't be a big radio hit, but such songs are possible. I remember singing them as a kid. I recall one that actually compared Christians to soldiers, marching as to war.

These classics are printed in a book called a "hymnal." Perhaps you've heard of these. You can buy one on eBay. Mine its rich lyrics, and then update the tunes for a modern audience. I'm telling you, the men will love it.

TOOL 12: THE JOURNEYS
ARE A TEMPLATE FOR PRAYER

Sometimes I pray according to the pattern of the journeys.

I begin with submission. I place my hands out in front of me, palms down. I imagine my cares, dreams, and possessions falling out of my hands and dropping at the feet of Jesus. This is a symbol of submission—of relinquishing control of everything to God. I tell him my problems and hand him my burdens. I confess my sins and ask his forgiveness.

Then I turn my palms up. This is a symbol of receiving strength from him. I ask him for everything I think I'll need that day. I ask for wisdom. Power. Guidance. Today's closing price of the stock market (just kidding).

Finally, I stretch out my hands to either side, as if I'm being crucified. I thank Christ for giving his life and ask him to make me a living sacrifice. I ask him to show me ways I can pour out my life for the benefit of others. I complete my prayer by asking him to guide me to the top of the mountain. I ask him for influence that extends beyond my natural life, and for a life that finishes well.

Chapter 18

MANLINESS VERSUS GODLINESS

The pews of America's churches were overflowing on Sunday, September 16, 2001. Five days earlier, the nation had been attacked. The Twin Towers of the World Trade Center were reduced to rubble. Millions flocked to houses of worship in search of comfort. In search of answers. In search of God.

I went to church that day. The pastor said something I'll never forget. "The Jesus in me says to love your enemies and to pray for those who persecute you. The Jesus in me proclaims, 'Do not resist an evil person,' and 'When a man strikes you on one cheek, turn to him the other also.'

"But the man in me wants to go out and kill someone. The man in me wants vengeance—swift, sweet vengeance— or at least a severe justice for these cold-blooded murderers who took so many innocent lives."

Have you experienced the tug-of-war between manliness and godliness? You want to do the things regular guys do, but you can't—because you're a Christian. Your heart tells you to behave a certain way, but your faith seems to command the opposite. Know what I'm talking about?

The church has been slow to recognize this tug-of-war. Rather than admit that Christian culture is becoming feminized, most preachers and teachers simply try to redefine manliness. To use a tug-of-war analogy, they try to move the line in the sand.

For example, if you attend a Christian men's rally, it won't be long before one of the speakers says something like this: "The world's definition of manliness is corrupt! Real manliness is not about being tough. It's about being weak, vulnerable, and dependent on God." Brandon O'Brien wrote in *Christianity Today*, "Humanity in the image of Christ is not aggressive and combative, it is humble and poor (Phillipians 2:5ff.). We are most like Christ not when we win a fight, but when we suffer for righteousness' sake (Ephesians 5:1–2; 1 Thessalonians 1:6; 2:14)."[1]

Are these men correct? Absolutely. But now that you're familiar with the three journeys, you can see what's happening. They're focusing exclusively on the first and third journeys, reducing the Christian faith to a religion relatively few men want to pursue.

———————

Most men are not aware of the tug-of-war. It plays out deep in our subconscious minds. It's not the big stuff that wears us down—it's those little, mundane decisions in which our faith and our hearts stand at odds.

Most followers of Jesus can identify the excesses that lie at either end of the manly-godly spectrum. Those are the easy calls. But what about the gray areas? Those daily decisions where our manhood and our faith might collide? Christian guys grapple with questions like these every day:

- How competitive can a Christian man be?
- Can I ever say a curse word?
- I think that guy is hitting on my girlfriend. Should I confront him?
- Do I speak the truth—even if it hurts feelings?
- Is it okay to go to a bar and have a beer after work?
- Can I ever lose my temper?
- Our new worship leader is so effeminate. Am I right to feel disgusted when he gets up to sing?
- Is it okay to drive a sports car?
- Can I just hang up on telemarketers, or do I have to be kind to them?
- I love late-night comedians, but some of their jokes are off-color. Can I still watch their shows?
- Do I have to hug guys at church?
- My teenager is showing disrespect. Should I respond with gentleness or toughness?
- How much sports is too much?
- My coworker is a racist. Is it wiser to confront him or to pray for him?
- My wife hasn't had sex with me in months. Can I demand it from her?
- There's this guy who wants to be my friend, but I don't like him. Is it okay to blow him off, or does Jesus require me to be his buddy?
- A bully is taunting my son. Should I tell him to fight back or to turn the other cheek?

The map can help in situations where the Bible is unclear or gives seemingly contradictory advice. It gives cautious men permission to be bolder, while showing forceful men when to temper their natural aggression. In short, the map can help men find a proper balance of masculinity and femininity in their lives.

Most important, the map helps men understand why their manhood is so stinkin' important in the first place. Let's go back to the very beginning of our journey to manhood. Look at the lower left corner of the map.

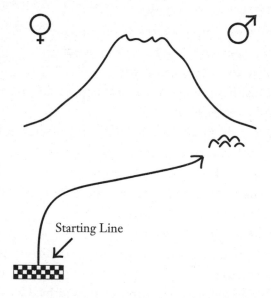

You began life as a female. So did Arnold Schwarzenegger, Nelson Mandela, Babe Ruth, Genghis Khan, Winston Churchill, Vince Lombardi, Gandhi, Sir Edmund Hillary, and Julius Caesar. Females, all.

Every egg is female, containing only the X chromosome common to women. So every human starts on the left side of the mountain, so to speak.

Meet Jack. He's a human egg. Excuse me, *she's* a human egg. But in a moment, a sperm will come knocking, bearing a Y chromosome. As soon as that sperm does its job, *she* is now a *he*. Jack has changed forever—from female to male.

Even though Jack is now biologically male, his psychological journey to manhood doesn't start right away. For nine months he is encased in a woman's body (it doesn't get any more female than that). He will spend his early years in a feminine world, in the company of babysitters, nursery school teachers, and, of course, his mom. During the preschool years he is only mildly aware of his gender, and this awareness has little effect on his behavior.

But when Jack reaches school age, something changes. One day he realizes that he can no longer play with his sister's dolls. He feels uncomfortable holding hands with another boy. He stops crying in public, no matter how bad it hurts. He no longer befriends girls; he persecutes them.

And with that, Jack's journey to manhood has begun. He has turned his back on all things feminine and set a course for masculinity—full speed ahead. By the time Jack is a teenager, manhood-seeking becomes his twenty-four-hour-a-day obsession. Like most young men, Jack does some unbelievably stupid things in high school and college just to prove to his peers how manly he is.

The natural journey to manhood leads Jack to a region known as the manly foothills. This is the false summit of manhood, adorned with chrome, camo, and gunmetal. The men who live here hang out in bars, barracks, bowling alleys, and boardrooms. They put fancy rims on their cars; they buy expensive toys; they get drunk on power; they use women and alcohol as anesthetics to dull their pain. They project a tough exterior to mask the weakness they feel inside.

You don't have to be a macho man to prowl these little hills—any bloke who worships his own freedom and autonomy will find a home here. Even guys who project a humble public image may be secret citizens of the manly foothills.

Some men never escape the foothills. They spend their entire lives camped here, proving themselves.

When Jack chooses to submit to God, it's much more than a religious decision. Psychologically, he's electing to do a 180—turning back in the direction he has been fleeing since childhood. Jack must willingly give up territory he has worked so diligently to conquer and must reapproach the feminine side. This is akin to a football player taking a handoff and rushing backward, toward his own end zone, yielding hard-earned yardage with every step.

No wonder Jack's friends think he's gone nuts.

What makes things worse, the church expects Jack to give up many of the habits that men enjoy—and to embrace behaviors that men associate with women.

I became a Christian during my teens. I immediately began "cleaning up my act." I stopped sneaking beer with my friends. No more cursing. Smoking was off-limits. I threw away my stash of *Playboy* magazines. Parties became a problem, since I had to be up early on Sunday. I even dumped my collection of rock-and-roll albums that promised to put me on the "highway to hell." And girls—beautiful, blossoming young women with boobs—I had to start treating them not as sex objects, but as sisters.

Most of these changes were right and necessary. Some were a bit too cautious (I sometimes miss those Led Zeppelin albums), but on the whole they did me good. They helped me get down off the foothills and set my feet on the mountain of manhood.

But as healthy as this movement was spiritually, it damaged me psychologically. As I took a broom to the unholy in my life, I inadvertently swept away many of the things that made me feel *manly*. I gave up the risky, devil-may-care habits that define young men. What's worse, I swapped these old routines for new ones that seemed rather feminine, family safe, and even wimpy. I stopped doing a bunch of guy things and started doing a bunch of girl things.

When you strip a man of the things that make him feel manly, he goes one of two ways: either he becomes passive and gets depressed (the Christian Nice Guy), or he compensates for the loss by cranking up the machismo.

This may be the underlying reason we have so many spiritually unhealthy men in the church. They know they're supposed to be both tough and tender, but they have no framework to help them juggle these competing demands. So they get stuck on the edges of the mountain.

———————

If you are a woman reading this, you may be wondering, Why don't men just get over themselves and stop worrying about their precious manhood? Why can't they get their self-image from their relationship with Jesus, and not from some psychological construct? They should just leave their need to be manly at the feet of Christ.

Sounds great, but you might as well ask a man to part with his testicles. The need to be manly is universal. And admit it, women: you prefer a man with a bit of swagger and self-confidence. A man cannot be emotionally healthy—and cannot satisfy a woman—if he does not think of himself as a proper man. The Bible challenges men to give up many things. Manhood is not on the list.

The last thing we want is for Christian men to cede more of their natural masculine tendencies. Those characteristics that make us squirm are the very things that bring strength to our churches, our families, and our communities, when properly channeled. Here are five ways the map can help men do this:

1. THE THREE JOURNEYS LET MEN DEVELOP BOTH SIDES OF THEIR PERSONALITIES

There's nothing worse than a feminized fellow—except perhaps a macho fool. The journeys help us avoid both extremes. Look again at the map:

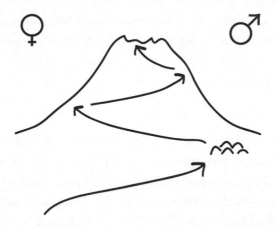

As we climb the mountain, we also move toward its center. Christian discipleship doesn't neuter the man, nor does it result in an androgynous hybrid of femininity and masculinity. A real man develops both his masculine and feminine gifts in full measure—just as Christ did.

2. THE MAP EXPLAINS CHRISTIANITY'S TOUGH-TENDER PARADOXES

The church seems to want it both ways. The man of God is supposed to be a warrior—who turns the other cheek. He's to take bold action—as he lets go and lets God. Dad is expected to step up and be the leader in his home, without imposing his will on his wife and children.

Adding to the confusion are Christian authors whose book titles encourage men to follow *The Barbarian Way*, to *Unleash Courageous Faith*, to *Risk*, and to become *Wild at Heart*.[2] After reading these books, we're ready to conquer the world! Then we come to church, where we're admonished to get along, be dependable, and never rock the boat.

A few years back Stu Weber wrote a popular men's book titled *Tender Warrior*.[3] That pretty much sums up the paradox in two words. *Tender warrior?* No wonder men sit in church and scratch their noggins.

What is the source of this spiritual schizophrenia? The Bible itself. Some Scripture passages encourage us to act a certain way, while others command the opposite. For example, Jesus tells his disciples to sell their cloaks and buy swords (Luke 22:36), yet that same evening he rebukes a disciple for wielding one (Matthew 26:52). In Ephesians 4:2, Paul pleads with us to walk in humility and gentleness, but two chapters later he tells us to prepare for battle. Christ told us to love our enemies, yet he was abrasive toward his.

Then there's the granddaddy of them all: the fruit of the Spirit paradox. In Galatians 5, the apostle Paul identifies love, joy, peace, patience, kindness, goodness, faithfulness, gentleness, and self-control as the marks of a Spirit-filled believer. But if this is the definitive test of Christian character, Jesus flunks on almost every count! Christ had a hot temper and regularly expressed *impatience* with his disciples (Matthew 17:17). He didn't show much *peace*, *gentleness*, or *self-control* while swinging that whip and overturning tables (Matthew 21:12–13). He hurled stinging insults at both friend and foe, words that were hardly *loving* or *kind* (Matthew 12:34 and many others). *Joy* eluded him as he neared the cross.

So what's going on? How could Jesus have acted the way he did—in clear violation of the teachings of Paul?

Once again, the map—and a little historical context—comes to the rescue. When Paul wrote the "fruit of the Spirit" passage to the Galatians, he was addressing a congregation of newborn Christians. First-journey Christians. (Galatians is believed to be Paul's earliest surviving epistle.) So naturally, he's pressing this church toward the softer virtues. But when the apostle writes to more mature believers, his rhetoric changes to that of strength. (Ephesians 6:10–20 is a good example. See also the epistles of Hebrews and James.) And consider Paul himself—a man on his third journey. What do you think God is whispering in his ear? *Sacrifice*. Many of his later writings (particularly his letters to Timothy) reflect the mind of a man who is preparing to be sacrificed: "For I am already being poured out like a drink offering, and the time has come for my departure. I have fought the good fight, I have finished the race, I have kept the faith" (2 Timothy 4:6–7).

So as you encounter clashing Bible passages, relax. When you see Christ acting in a manner that seems un-Christlike (if this were possible), now you understand. Jesus' actions were always consistent with the journey he was traveling.

And the commands given in the Epistles reflect the spiritual journey of the people to whom they're addressed.

3. THE THREE JOURNEYS HELP US UNDERSTAND OUR FEMINIZED CHURCH CULTURE

My first book, *Why Men Hate Going to Church*, was all about the feminization of the church. One of the reasons men are becoming disenchanted with Christianity is because its culture is becoming so feminine.

But now that I've discovered the three journeys, I find the rising tide of estrogen a little more bearable. I understand the motivation of today's preachers, teachers, and musicians. Why do they skew their ministry toward feminine themes? Because the pews are filled with rookie Christians. Fresh recruits need movement in the feminine direction—and that's what we give them, week after week.

So if you're sitting in church and the music sounds like a Top 40 love song to Jesus, take a deep breath. If the preacher begs you to "experience God's tender embrace," chill. When some guy gets up and starts blubbering like a girl during his testimony, lighten up. You may not like it, but the feminine journey is part of the deal. We'll tackle this issue headlong in the next chapter.

4. THE MAP SHOWS WHY REVIVALS AND RETREATS ARE SUCH HOTBEDS OF EMOTION

Have you ever attended an old-fashioned tent revival? Emotions run high, to say the least. Or how about a spiritual retreat such as Cursillo or Walk to Emmaus? You'll find lots of introspection, sharing in small groups, supportive conversation, and, of course, hugs. There's always a box of Kleenex at Cursillo.

Now you know why. Revivals and retreats are designed to help people surrender to God. That means leaving the foothills behind and walking in submission. Therefore, it's perfectly natural that these events will have a feminine feel. If you attend a revival or a retreat, be prepared for a weekend dominated by feminine themes and imagery. Lots of support. Emotion. Weeping.

The next time you find yourself in one of these emotional hothouses, don't take it as an affront to your manliness. Instead, see it as an opportunity to resubmit your heart to Christ and to prepare yourself for the third journey.

5. THE THREE JOURNEYS ARE WRITTEN ON THE HEART OF EVERY MAN

Do you watch guy movies? If so, you've seen the three journeys played out many times on the silver screen. See if this plotline sounds familiar: A cocky young stud decides to confront some evil in his own strength. He's nearly killed by the bad guys. Suddenly an aged, wrinkled man shows up and gives the villains a whuppin'. The old coot offers to train the immature hothead. The student humbles himself and accepts the training of the master (submission). He develops true physical and mental toughness (strength). Eventually our young hero meets his adversary and, after a back-and-forth battle, defeats him in spectacular fashion, sometimes dying in the process (sacrifice).

Men around the globe trek by the millions to theaters to

watch the three journeys acted out on the big screen. Why do we love this story? Because God branded it onto our souls. Every man longs to walk these ancient paths, whether he realizes it or not.

Chapter 19

THE THREE JOURNEYS
AT CHURCH

Kurt is a committed Christian who can hardly stand to attend worship services anymore. He's not sure why. "I feel I can actually serve God better if I don't waste my time at church." Stan recently left his longtime church for another. "The messages seemed very basic," he says. "I just wasn't being fed." Bert is a former deacon who has stopped attending church altogether. "I'm tired of *going* to church. I want to *be* the church."

Even as churches become more hip and relevant, more focused on our "felt needs," more open and accepting, men are falling away. Even as youth groups become more "worshipful" and "authentic," boys are falling away. (So are women and girls, but in smaller numbers.) Churches are studying and polling us, finding out what we want and presenting the gospel to us the way we say we want it—but then we turn and trample this pearly package underfoot. The percentage of Americans who identify themselves as Christians shrinks each year.

What is the source of this sickness? Why is it spreading through our congregations? The three journeys may point us to the answer.

About a year ago, I started corresponding with a guy named Roger. He has been a Christian for many years, and he's established in a growing church he really likes. "They are so creative. They're never stuffy or religious," he says. "The music is top quality. The preaching is dynamic and always includes Scripture. I have many great friends at church. In all honesty, this is the congregation I've been looking for my whole life. It fits me to a T."

But lately Roger has been losing his enthusiasm for worship services. "I don't think the problem is feminization," he says. "They do a very good job incorporating the masculine spirit in worship. They even avoid those lovey-dovey praise songs," he says with a laugh. "But rarely do I leave the church feeling inspired. There's something lacking, but I just can't put my finger on it."

Roger and I exchanged a few more e-mails, and then he asked me what I was writing. I shared the three journeys with him and showed him an early sketch of the map.

The following Sunday Roger wrote me an e-mail brimming with excitement. "I just figured out what the problem is!" he exclaimed. "My church is completely focused on the journey of submission. Even though we target men, we're constantly pushing people toward a feminine spiritual journey. I finally see it.

"Our associate pastor spoke today," Roger continued. "He used the word *brokenness* forty-two times in a thirty-minute sermon. We offer support groups of every kind. Then I noticed our church's marketing slogan: 'It's not about rules. It's about relationships.'"

Roger logged onto his church's Web site and looked back

at the sermon topics. Over the past three years, his church had presented multiple sermons on relationships. On God's grace. His comfort for the weary, burdened, and hurting. His acceptance of us—just as we are. But only twice in that three-year period had his pastor preached anything related to strength.

"It's almost as if they're afraid to present this side of Christianity," Roger wrote. "I can see why it might be important to focus on submission for the sake of new believers. But for a guy like me who's been walking with Christ for thirty years, it's old news. I'm well acquainted with God's love, grace, and forgiveness. I'm not trying to work my way to heaven. I'm no longer racked with guilt over past sins. My marriage is incredibly rich."

Roger concluded his e-mail this way: "I know this sounds arrogant, but I say it in all humility: submission is not where I'm at anymore. God broke this stallion a long time ago."

Roger is not the only guy in his church who feels this way. A number of men (and women) are quietly asking for "meatier" teaching. God is calling the maturing men of the congregation to a journey of strength. They're searching for God the Father, not God our comforting Mother. Mark Galli writes in *Christianity Today*:

> Many churches are growing because they preach a God of second and third and fourth chances, and a faith that gives palpable hope, joy, and acceptance. What's not to like? Indeed, there are gracious aspects of the Christian faith. But let's face it, the word *strict* does not apply. The Jesus who tells followers to sever offending hands, to let the dead bury themselves, to give one's possessions to the poor, to take up the cross—well, he's not easy to find in our churches these days.[1]

It's not just the seeker-friendly churches that have locked away second-journey Jesus in the attic like some crazy uncle. The liberal mainline began hiding him in the 1950s. Pentecostals are toning him down. Even Baptist churches are focusing less on heaven and hell and more on the here and now.

Why this shift? It's not some satanic plot. No, our congregations are simply responding to the real needs of real people. Let me break it down for you:

- Most churchgoers are immature.
- Immature believers and nonbelievers need the lessons of submission.
- So we focus the bulk of our teaching and music on the first journey.

On the one hand, this strategy makes perfect sense. The only way to grow a church without stealing from other congregations is to focus on the unchurched. And if we're going to "make disciples," we must start with the immature. Therefore, we provide milk, since you can't feed steak to a newborn babe.

But on the other hand, as we nurse these young Christians, we starve maturing men like Roger and give all the men the false impression that Christianity is a one-way trip to girly-town. When we preach, teach, and sing the first journey week after week, we unwittingly weaken the men—and feminize the church. Here's a little story to illustrate.

Larry grew up in a conservative evangelical church where Jesus was presented as a rather stern, demanding Savior.

Larry's boyhood pastor was a verse-by-verse, expository preacher who spoke a language called Christianese. His messages were often dull (you try to squeeze a good talk out of Leviticus 2). Larry's pastor made up for his lack of inspiration by pounding the pulpit, raising his voice, and gesturing. Every Sunday he waved his Bible in the air, its gold-leaf edges shimmering like a lure in search of a trout.

Every service ended with an altar call, an opportunity to escape the flames of hell by receiving Christ as personal Lord and Savior. Although congregants were regularly challenged to "win the world for Jesus," in reality there was little outreach beyond the once-a-year Vacation Bible school. Even as a boy Larry was concerned about his friends' salvation. He invited many to come to church, but none ever came back. Young Larry was frustrated—his friends needed to know Jesus, but they simply couldn't relate to his congregation's odd subculture.

Larry grew up and heard God's call to the ministry. He decided to become a church planter, and now he's determined to not repeat these mistakes. Like Rick Warren, Bill Hybels, and other well-known megachurch leaders, he has decided to target the unchurched. Larry wants his congregation to be a hospital for sinners, not a museum for saints.

Pastor Larry launches his new church (Grace Fellowship) in a school gym. He works hard to bring in the irreligious. He prays earnestly. God answers his prayers, and soon he has a nursery full of "babes in Christ."

Larry doesn't know about the three journeys, but he instinctively begins emphasizing the journey of submission. After all, his congregation is full of barely Christian people. So he teaches the basics: the Sermon on the Mount, the fruit of the Spirit, and the doctrine of grace. Larry's sermons slowly convince his flock that God is not angry or judgmental. He never preaches a sermon that doesn't mention God's love and mercy.

Pastor Larry is a captivating speaker. More and more people come to hear his messages of hope, grace, and forgiveness. God blesses Grace Fellowship, which is soon running four Sunday services in the school gym. The church starts raising money for land and a building.

Grace Fellowship continues to emphasize the first journey, and the crowds swell even more. After eight long years, the church finally moves into its shiny new building. Then another brilliant move: Larry hires a worship leader from Hillsong Church in Australia. Not only is Jerome a talented performer, but he understands the needs of seekers. Larry and Jerome synchronize the music and preaching around the themes of brokenness, surrender, and our love relationship with Jesus. The church clicks past two thousand and then three thousand in weekly attendance.

All these new Christians and pre-Christians bring heavy burdens and hurts. Larry responds with sermons based on their needs. In June he preaches a series titled "Jesus on Relationships." Then it's six weeks in Galatians: "God's Comforting Grace." His next series is titled "Lay Your Burden Down." Come autumn, Larry preaches Rick Warren's "Forty Days of Love." Larry is careful to buttress his sermons with Scripture. The weekly PowerPoint presentation always includes at least a half dozen verses plucked from various translations of the Bible.

Soon Grace Fellowship crashes through the five-thousand-attendee mark. There's talk of launching satellite campuses via live video feed. The church offers support groups of every kind. Testimonies pour in from grateful individuals who have been touched by the compassionate ministry of the church. Larry has what he prayed for: a hospital for sinners.

Everything seems to be going remarkably well, but soon some cracks appear. The church conducts a survey and finds huge turnover. Grace Fellowship attracts lots of visitors, but almost three-quarters of its new members disappear within a year. Longtime members are also drifting away. It's hard to find spiritually mature workers to run the church's sprawling ministry programs. Men are becoming less involved. The volunteer corps runs two-thirds female, and 70 percent of the seniors in the high school youth group are girls. Giving wobbles. Less than 5 percent of the church's multimillion-dollar budget goes for off-campus missions and outreach.

Most disturbing of all, Pastor Larry is beginning to realize that Grace Fellowship is very good at filling chairs, but not so good at making committed disciples who truly live for Christ. Larry recently attended a Reveal Conference at which his hero, Bill Hybels, founding pastor of Willow Creek Church, admitted the same.[2] Hybels surveyed his congregation of more than twenty thousand attendees and found that "pre-Christians, or people who are still seeking and exploring Christianity, rated the church 'very high.' Ratings dropped slightly among new Christians but were still 'fantastic.' Adolescent Christians rated the church as 'good.' But fully devoted followers of Christ indicated less satisfaction, saying they are not sure the church is helping them as much at this stage in their life."[3] Almost a quarter of Willow's members admitted they were stalled in their spiritual growth and were thinking about leaving the church. The most mature Christians clamored for "much more depth and challenge from the services."[4]

Ever since the Reveal Conference, Pastor Larry has been

staying up nights, praying about this conundrum, feeling trapped. He's still committed to reaching the unchurched. He's certain that the hellfire-and-brimstone preaching he grew up with is not the answer, yet there was something about it that worked. After all, it convinced Larry to leave everything and follow Christ. Larry ends each day with this prayer: "Lord, how can Grace Fellowship be a church that reaches both the immature and the mature in Christ?"

Fast-growing churches like Grace Fellowship are often criticized for preaching a watered-down gospel. They're slammed because their teaching isn't "deep enough." But I disagree. Any sermon that's rooted in Scripture is plenty deep.

The problem is not depth but breadth. By downplaying the second journey, pastors like Larry are unwittingly depriving their flocks of the fullness of Christ. To use a couple of food metaphors, Larry is feeding his people appetizers and dessert but is withholding the main course. Second-journey teachings are like canned spinach. They're often slimy and tough to swallow, but they build muscle—especially in men.

Now back to Larry. He has done an excellent job instructing the men of his congregation on submission. His therapeutic messages have led many men to seek healing. These guys have conquered habitual sins that once held them captive. Their lives aren't perfect, but they're basically aligned with God's will.

So every Sunday the chairs of Grace Fellowship are sprinkled with men who have walked the journey of submission. Tell me, what is God likely to call these men to next? Yep—a journey of strength. And that's exactly what's happening at Grace. God is whispering to the men of the church.

Several are sensing a holy nudging toward something else—something bigger, wilder, and more dangerous—but they don't know what it is. They're thinking, *Okay, I'm healed. Now what?*

These men sit quietly every Sunday, listening to sermons that teach them how to fight battles they won long ago. They volunteer in the church—parking cars, passing out bulletins, and changing diapers—but frustration begins to mount. They know their training as disciples is not complete, yet they have no way to discover the next step. Grace Fellowship doesn't teach the second journey, nor does it help people transition from submission to strength. Frankly, Pastor Larry doesn't even know about this transition, because he has never heard of the three journeys.

Larry desperately wants faithful, strong men at Grace Fellowship. Yet the church's heavy emphasis on submission makes it almost impossible for the men to transition to an active, bold faith. The men of Grace Fellowship want to be "wild at heart" like second-journey Jesus, but they have no idea how to do this in a healthy manner.[5]

———

So what advice would you give Larry? Many would say, "He should forget that felt-needs stuff. Just preach the Word and let the chips fall where they may. After all, the Bible says, 'All Scripture is given by inspiration of God, and is profitable for doctrine, for reproof, for correction, for instruction in righteousness, that the man of God may be complete, thoroughly equipped for every good work'" (2 Timothy 3:16–17 NKJV).

On the one hand, this is absolutely true. I have seen simple, straightforward Bible teaching accomplish amazing things in people's lives. When we cherry-pick the Scriptures, it's almost as if we're repackaging God to make him more palatable to the masses.

But on the other hand, you can't argue with results. By emphasizing the tender, compassionate, sunny side of Jesus, contemporary churches have brought millions of skittish people into contact with a loving God. These congregations may be "a mile wide and an inch deep," but at least they're bringing in new folks.

Frankly, I don't see anything wrong with emphasizing the kinder, gentler, and more loving aspects of the gospel in weekly public worship. When it comes to unbelievers and young believers, carrots are more effective than sticks. It is God's kindness—not his judgment—that leads to repentance (Romans 2:4). The old evangelistic strategy of "scaring the hell out of people" simply does not work in today's world.

However, if we're going to emphasize the first journey in public preaching, then we need an alternative way to introduce the second journey to those who are ready for it.

I think the best place to teach strength is in a small group of men who know and trust each other. Even postmoderns will accept lessons on hell, condemnation, and persecution if the "bad news" is delivered in a small group. Challenges to a person's lifestyle from the pulpit can sound judgmental and narrow-minded, but the same exhortation delivered in a small group of friends will come across as caring. A man will accept challenging doctrine more readily from a friend sitting beside him than from a pastor standing over him.

Now I'm going to go controversial on you. If Sunday morning worship services are going to target seekers and young Christians, then we need to excuse the mature from attending them. Yes, that's what I said. At some point we need to let people "graduate" from the weekly worship service.

I know—this sounds like heresy. But whether we like it or not, this is happening already. I know many highly committed men (deacons, elders, and even pastors) who are abandoning institutional churches, not because they're running from God, but because they want *more* of him. John Eldredge has noticed the trend as well:

> We've spoken to a number of good people, mature believers who sincerely love God and dearly want to join him in his battle for this world, but who have found church to be an exercise in frustration. The number of these folks continues to grow; it is a very significant trend. These are not simply malcontents, who really just want to sleep in on Sundays. These are sincere followers of Jesus and they want a genuine place of church; they just don't know where to find it.[6]

These restless men (and women) are simply being honest: church attendance does little to grow their faith. They're no longer searching for a "better" church, because they've realized that a weekly worship service will never deliver what their hearts long for. Instead, these guys are cobbling together a spiritual life based on personal devotions, fellowship with other believers, service, and giving. They listen to podcasts from the handful of pastors who have the courage to teach the second and third journeys. These dudes are more than willing to invest in their faith, but they don't want to sit at base camp. They want to climb.

If local churches want to retain and deploy their maturing men, they need to develop an intentional, rigorous discipleship regimen that will help these fellows walk the journey of strength. Bill Hybels has responded to Willow Creek's discipleship crisis by offering seminary-level Bible classes on Wednesday nights. (I'm not sure you can produce disciples in a classroom, but at least Willow is trying something different.) Other churches and parachurch organizations are offering "life coaching" sessions in which believers challenge each other in their journeys of strength.

I am working on this very issue now. Together with other like-minded men, I'm developing a discipleship curriculum based on the three journeys. The curriculum trains spiritually mature men to go back down the mountain and help the younger ones find their way to the top. If you'd like to check my progress, visit www.threejourneys.com.

This new curriculum is different from anything I've seen. It is not a book study. You don't have to read anything. No filling in blanks. Instead, we're attempting to make disciples the way Jesus did: by leading men through a series of experiences that bring the journeys alive.

Is it even possible to disciple modern men the way Jesus did? The way Gerasimos discipled me? We'll see in our next chapter.

Chapter 20

FINDING GERASIMOS

This book is almost finished, so I have a little parting gift
for you:

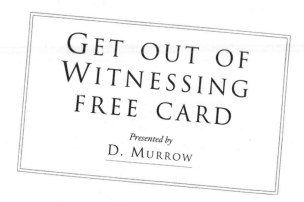

GET OUT OF
WITNESSING
FREE CARD

Presented by
D. MURROW

I have another confession to make: I'm an absolutely
lousy evangelist. I've never won a stranger to Christ. It's
weird—I'm a pretty good salesman, but when I try to "sell
Jesus," I fall flat. I simply have no gift for soul winning.

When my pastor boards an airplane, it seems like he's

always seated next to a person in crisis. He simply utters the name of Jesus, and before the flight attendant wraps up the safety briefing, his seatmate is sobbing, repenting, and on his way to heaven. Me? The moment I mention I'm a Christian, my seatmate dives for the in-flight magazine. Conversation over.

Over the years, I've felt a mixture of guilt and inadequacy over my lack of skill as a cold-call evangelist. But in studying the journey of sacrifice, I've found some encouragement from Jesus. Here is his final commandment to us:

> Go therefore and *make disciples* of all the nations, baptizing them in the name of the Father and of the Son and of the Holy Spirit, teaching them to observe all things that I have commanded you; and lo, I am with you always, even to the end of the age. (Matthew 28:19–20 NKJV; emphasis added)

Look closely. Jesus does not say, "Go therefore and make converts." He ordered us to *make disciples*. That means there's hope for people like me, because even an inept evangelist can make a disciple. While potential converts may be few and far between, potential disciples are everywhere you look (John 4:35).

MAKE DISCIPLES IN CHURCH

Your congregation is full of men who are waiting to be discipled. Deep in their hearts, these men are looking for Gerasimos. They secretly long for a mentor who will love them the way the monk loved me—by exposing my hypocrisy, smashing my false perceptions, and challenging me to go higher.

Practically every man in your congregation is stuck some-where on the mountain. All they need is a push from another man who cares.

Think what would happen in your church if every man were being personally discipled by another. I suspect many of the problems we deal with in our churches and families would quickly evaporate. If men had spiritual fathers, would we even need women's ministry or children's ministry?

MAKE DISCIPLES AT WORK

Think about the guys you work with. Maybe a fellow employee is wandering the manly foothills. He might not go to church with you, but he'd probably go to lunch. Order a couple of burgers and let him talk. You don't have to convert him—just listen.

If the opportunity presents itself, tell him about the journeys. "Hey, I'm reading this interesting book about manhood. It says that every great man walks three journeys in his life." Then grab a napkin and draw him the map. Ask him where he thinks he is on the mountain. If he's a typi-cal guy, he'll appreciate seeing his journey to manhood in visual form.

MAKE DISCIPLES AT PLAY

The three journeys allow you to have a deeply spiritual con-versation without even mentioning religion. You can present the journeys to your friends as the key to success in any human endeavor, from work to warfare. If your friend asks you how you discovered the map, show him this book, or tell him, "It comes from the Bible."

Disciple making doesn't require you to witness on street corners, travel to Africa, or pass out tracts at the county fair. You don't have to lead a Bible study or preach a sermon. Disciple making is the ancient art of kicking a man in the pants—in love. You can disciple any man, whether he's a longtime Christian or a total atheist. Who knows, you might accidentally lead one to faith in Jesus.

A church that makes disciples won't have to worry about evangelism, because conversions will happen naturally. They may be fewer in number, but there will also be fewer false conversions. And fewer young believers will fall through the cracks.

So many of our Christian activities generate a short-term buzz. Revivals, rallies, retreats, concerts, and worship events have the power to excite us for a day or two, but the glow quickly fades. Disciple making lacks the flash of these catalytic events, but it has lasting impact.

When I speak to groups of men, I often ask, "Have you ever been personally discipled by another man?" About 20 percent of the hands go up. Then I ask, "What was it like?" Words like *awesome*, *life changing*, and *challenging* flow from their lips. Many men say something like this: "It made all the difference in my life. Nothing else comes close."

How can you find a Gerasimos? Ask God. Perhaps a mentor like Gerasimos is sitting in your congregation. Find out if there is a man in your church or community who mentors other men. Gerasimos often works quietly, under the radar.

He's probably willing to take you on as a disciple, but you must ask.

If no one in your congregation is doing this kind of mentoring, you can approach a mature Christian man you admire. Ask him straight up: "Will you mentor me?" Tell him you'd like to meet him weekly for a couple of months to talk about how to follow Jesus. Give him a copy of this book to show him what you're aiming for. You may end up changing his life as much as he changes yours. (If he doesn't know how to disciple you, he can visit my Web site, www.threejourneys.com, for ideas.)

———————

How can you *become* a Gerasimos? I'm convinced that God is calling many men to be disciple makers, but they're afraid. They wonder:

- Who am I to do this? I'm unqualified.
- I might get in over my head.
- I'm afraid of messing up.
- I don't know the Bible well enough.
- I won't know what to say.
- It might become a giant time-suck.
- What if I over-challenge a guy and he drops out of the church or renounces his faith?
- My church offers no training or support for disciple makers.
- I've never been discipled myself. How can I be a spiritual father when I've never had one?

These fears are valid—yet Christ calls us to make disciples anyway. If you decide to disciple men, things will go wrong.

It will get messy. You'll get in over your head. Guaranteed. But do it anyway. If you remain rooted in submission and draw your strength from God, then Christ will be with you as you sacrifice your life for other men.

Here are some ideas (in no particular order):

- *Locate a church that supports disciple makers*. Don't go into this kind of work alone. It's hard. You need help.
- *Work with a partner who has a similar vision*. Find another man in the church who wants to make disciples, and labor together.
- *When seeking disciples, look for men in transition* (loss of a job, loss of a loved one, etc.). These fellows tend to be less busy and more open to turning a corner in their lives.
- *Seek men who have potential*. Jesus didn't take every man into his inner circle. He handpicked his disciples because he saw something special in them.
- *Learn to listen*. Disciple makers are not teachers; they're mentors. They use their ears more than their mouths.
- *Learn to ask great questions*. Questions open a man up; answers shut him down.
- *Do things with men*. Guys often feel freer to talk while doing something else. Men bond side by side rather than face-to-face.
- *After you've gotten to know a man, ask his permission to challenge him*. Most men will say yes instantly. Then do it!
- *Keep your disciples off balance*. Surprise them regularly.

- *Most important, remember that discipleship is not a classroom experience.* Let me hit that last one again: discipleship cannot come about by reading a book. It is not Bible study, Sunday school, churchgoing, or seminary. It's not a retreat or a revival.

People send men's discipleship material to me all the time. "Hey, Dave," they say, "we've got this great new discipleship program for men!" But when I look it over, I'm always disappointed, because it's not discipleship at all. It's a Bible study course. The idea is to get men to read their Bibles (which most of them forget to do) and then gather them in an informal classroom setting (a living room) where they read from books and answer questions. You've attended these groups. The format is always the same: Bibles, books, banter, and a bowl of chips.

What if the military trained soldiers the way the church trains disciples? No more crack-of-dawn calisthenics, bellowing drill sergeants, or twenty-mile hikes. Instead, young GIs would sit in a circle and study books about war, sharing their opinions and validating each other's experiences. Then it's off to sensitivity training, conflict resolution, and a weekend retreat to sing military songs and listen to a general.

A disciple maker is more of a drill sergeant than a classroom teacher. His goal is to not produce students who hold great opinions, but soldiers who perform great deeds.

Recall how Gerasimos discipled me. He rebuked me. He kept me off balance so that I was always wondering what was coming next. There was a bit of tension and mystery in our relationship. We were not pals: he was the teacher, and I was the student. Gerasimos had a clear vision of where he wanted me to go. He led me through a series of life-changing experiences, rather than through a stack of books. He involved my body—not just my mind—in the discipleship process.

Funny. That's exactly how Jesus trained his men. As I look at the Gospels, I don't see Christ handing out study guides to the Twelve. No fill-in-the-blanks. No Doritos. Jesus taught his men by doing stuff with them. Then he used those experiences to change their lives.

Hear me: I'm not anti–Bible study. A good discipler will always point his men back to the Scriptures. But men will not become true disciples through study alone, because words cannot penetrate the deepest recesses of a man's soul. It is good for a man to read God's Word, but he is transformed when he *experiences* God's Word.

As you take on the challenge of discipling a man, you can do it "the usual way." You can fire random Bible lessons at him. You can use a topical study guide. Or you can lead him through the three journeys, in the proper order. Which method do you think will work best?

As I mentioned in the previous chapter, I'm working with a team of men to produce a discipleship regimen that follows Matthew's map. Visit www.threejourneys.com to learn more.

THE CALL

Yellow leaves fluttered from the arms of a gleaming white birch. They fell lazily to the earth, dappling my frost-covered lawn with drops of gold. It was autumn in Alaska—the air was dry, but all creation was moist. The earth and everything in it were preparing for six months of snow and cold.

I had just returned from a brisk morning walk when the phone rang. At first I heard nothing, and I assumed it was one of those computer-generated sales calls. Then a robust voice crackled over the line.

"David? This is Gerasimos."

"Teacher! It's been a long time. How are you? *Where* are you?"

"I am fine, and I am in Israel. At this moment I am walking around Jerusalem. This is the first time I've used a mobile phone."

In my mind's eye I saw an image of a bearded, black-clad monk cruising the streets of the Old City with a cell phone stuck to his ear. "Why are you in Israel?" I asked.

"I've joined the Russian abbot, Pavel, and Nikolai on a pilgrimage to the Holy Land. I'm having a marvelous time walking in the footsteps of Christ. All expenses paid."

I laughed aloud. "It's so good to hear your voice."

And with that, the small talk was over. "David, the Lord has brought you to my mind over the past few days. Is everything all right?"

"Yes, Teacher, everything is fine. The book is doing well, but lately it has been generating some tough questions. Things I didn't anticipate. Can I ask you about them?"

"Yes, of course. I am borrowing the abbot's phone, and he told me to talk as long as I liked."

Yikes! A mobile call on a Greek phone, originating from Israel? I tried not to think about how much these minutes were costing. "Gerasimos, as I speak about the three journeys, women get very excited too. Naturally, they ask, 'What about us? What does a woman's journey look like?'"

"I have pondered this at length," said the monk. "I'm sure that women have a mountain to conquer—and that they are required to walk three journeys. But in what order? And in which direction? Does the masculine come first? Justus of Sidon did not address this in his manuscript. And while there are many great women in Scripture, few of their stories are told in detail."

"So you're saying you don't know?"

The monk paused. "I have an idea, but I must talk to the Lord about it first. If he tells me something exciting, I'll share it with you, and you can make it into another bestseller." I heard a smile in his voice. The vacation was obviously doing him some good.

"Teacher, I have another question. Some of the men who are discussing the map say they feel pressured by the journeys. They think it's one more thing to add to their spiritual to-do list."

"These men are fools," the monk snapped. "Would a

traveler say, 'I feel so burdened by this map in my knapsack. Pity me! If I get lost, I'll have to pull it out and read it'?" The monk raised his voice. "The map is a tool and nothing more. Would a carpenter say, 'I have a new saw. Now I feel pressure to use it. What a burden on me'?"

I smiled. I missed Gerasimos's dry wit and sharp tongue. Over the line I heard about ten seconds of muffled coughing. "Excuse me, David; it's very dry and dusty here." The monk cleared his throat and continued. "The three journeys are not an obligation for a man to fulfill. They exist for one purpose: to benefit ordinary males who want to become extraordinary men. They do not create pressure; they relieve the pressure a man feels when he wanders aimlessly through life."

As the monk was speaking, I grabbed a pen and began jotting notes on the back of an envelope. I thought, *Why is there never decent paper when I'm learning from Gerasimos?*

"David, how are men reacting to the teaching?" Gerasimos asked. "Do they understand the journeys?"

"Some do," I said. "But I've noticed something odd: almost every man claims to be on the journey of submission. Hardly anyone wants to admit he's walking in strength or sacrifice. Even committed Christian men who are doing great things seem to underestimate their progress up the mountain."

The monk seemed to have anticipated my question. "David, let's say you meet a man of the church, and after a few minutes he looks you in the eye and says, 'You know, my faith is very strong.' What would you think of such a man?"

"He sounds rather egotistical," I said.

"Exactly. We teach Christian men to be modest and humble. To say, 'I'm walking in strength,' sounds like boasting to our church-trained ears. It's almost as if men are afraid God will smite them for being arrogant. So to be safe before God and acceptable to their peers, men humbly place themselves in the first journey, even though they are further along—and they know it."

"You know, you're right," I said. "I've noticed that Christian men tend to hide their strengths and advertise their weaknesses. So, Teacher, what would you say to these men?"

"I would rebuke them. Point out their false humility. It's pride in disguise. Tell them the truth—God wants his sons to be strong, powerful, and dangerous. And he doesn't care if others know it."

As I was musing, the monk kept right on teaching. "False humility is a problem, but so is false superiority."

"What do you mean?" I asked.

"Men will turn anything into a competition—even the spiritual life. A man should never use his position on the mountain to make another disciple feel inferior—or to make himself feel superior to another. The journeys do not describe our virtue, but our progress."

I had the phone cradled on my left shoulder as I furiously took notes with my right hand. "One more question for you, Teacher. I meet a lot of men who are unable to identify what journey they're on. They see the map and they understand the concept, but they have a tough time placing themselves on the mountain."

"There are three possibilities," Gerasimos said. "First, some men may not care what journey they're on. They may be comfortable with their faith walk as it is and feel no need for a map. As long as they're advancing, the tools they use do not matter.

"Now the second possibility. Some men may never have thought of having a map of their spiritual lives. It may take these fellows some time and discernment to identify their position. They should be asking God every day to help them find their place on the mountain.

"Then there is a third possibility," he said. "Some men may not be on the mountain at all. They may still be in the foothills and not realize it."

The monk coughed again and then continued. "Even devout, religious men can be deceived. I know monks who have given up everything, yet I sense in my spirit that they are not truly walking with Christ. Don't you remember what Jesus said? At the judgment there will be men who performed miracles in his name, yet on that terrible day he will turn to them and say, 'I never knew you. Away from me, you evildoers!'"

I said nothing, so Gerasimos continued. "David, do you recall the clue from the Sermon on the Mount?"

"You mean the passage that pointed Justus toward the map?"

"Yes, Matthew chapter 7, verses 13 and 14. Please recite these for me."

He thinks I have the chapter memorized. "Give me a moment, Teacher." Fortunately, my wife had left her Bible on the kitchen counter. I flipped to Matthew and read the verses into the telephone: "'Enter through the narrow gate. For wide is the gate and broad is the road that leads to destruction, and many enter through it. But small is the gate and narrow the road that leads to life, and only a few find it.'"

As I finished reading, Gerasimos pounced. "David, your book focuses on the road—the path that leads up the mountain. But tell me—where does the road begin?"

I looked back at the verse. Slowly I recited its first five words: "Enter through the narrow gate." I swallowed hard. *How did I miss this?*

The monk's voice took on a grave tone. "There is only

one access point to the mountain. Christ refers to it as 'the gate.' So, David, what is this gate Jesus is talking about?"

I was confused and embarrassed. I'd written an entire book based on a single passage of Scripture, and now I realized I'd left out the most important detail. *What is the gate?* "I don't know, Teacher. Please—tell me."

Gerasimos was silent for a moment. I was prepared for a sharp reproof, but instead he responded with patience. "In John chapter 10, verse 9, Jesus says, 'I am the gate; whoever enters through me will be saved.'

"This is what separates the disciples of Jesus from those who pursue other religions. Many faiths have great teachings. All bear valuable truths. But Christ boldly declares that *he* is the narrow gate. Not his teachings. Not his sacraments. Not even his church. Christ is the gate. And we do not set foot on the mountain of manhood until we go through him."

How did I miss the gate? I had a sick feeling in the pit of my stomach—the one you get when you arrive at class and realize there's a test you forgot to study for.

Gerasimos was not done. "David, find your copy of the map. Draw an arrow leading men down off the foothills. At the base of the foothills draw a small gate. Label it 'The Gate of Surrender.'"

"This gate is where the three journeys must begin,"

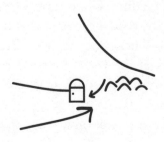

Gerasimos said. "Yet even many religious men have never entered the gate. They've been baptized. They've learned the prayers. They may have done penance or prayed at an altar. But they have never entered the gate. Such men think they are climbing the mountain, but in reality they are standing on a religious foothill.

"Other men are irreligious—and proud of it. They wander around the foothills, trying to be good men. They think of themselves as spiritual, whatever that means. They end up on the broad road that leads to destruction, not because they are bad men, but because they have failed to look for the narrow road, due to laziness or arrogance."

"Gerasimos, what is the broad road? It's not on the map."

"The broad road is many things. It is any human-made path to happiness. It is the foothills; it is the base of the mountain; it is any route that attempts to bypass the gate. Jesus was right: the men who travel this broad road end up destroying their lives, their families, and their potential as human beings."

"So this gate—it's a fourth journey?"

"No, my son. The gate of surrender is not a journey; it is a decision. A journey takes years, but a decision is made in a moment. Once a man decides to surrender, the three journeys become available to him. Hear me: a man cannot even begin the three journeys until he enters through the narrow gate—Christ himself. Jesus warned us that anyone who tries to bypass the gate is a thief and a robber."

"But didn't you say that irreligious men could also walk the three journeys?"

"There have been great men who have achieved much without walking through the gate. Their lives have roughly conformed to the pattern. But haven't you noticed—these talented men often lead destructive private lives. So tell me—which road are they on?"

"The broad one, I suppose," I said.

"Jesus was clear: this earthly life is not about personal achievement. He said, 'What does it profit a man if he gains the whole world but loses his soul?' This is why it's essential to pass through the gate. As you do so, a part of Christ 'sticks' to you. This sticky part is called the Holy Spirit and stays with you forever. Now you carry with you an internal Guide who shows you how to climb and where to go. He lifts your pack when it becomes too heavy. He gives you direction and confidence as you climb. Only a fool would attempt to conquer this mountain without the Guide."

I flashed back to *my* gate of surrender. I was a miserable fifteen-year-old who was out of answers. Even at this young age, I knew I was on the broad road that leads to destruction. I remember kneeling by the side of my bed and praying these words: "God, I'm messing up my life. From now on you're the boss. I give up—I'm all yours." It was indeed a moment of surrender. I stood up from that brief prayer— and I was a different man. My heart was lifted. My feet were on the mountain. I had walked through the gate.

"David, you must tell men that the gate is the only access point to the mountain. Look at them and say, 'Get down off your foothill. You must descend before you can rise. Once you are low, walk up to the gate and humbly ask Jesus if you may enter there. Be prepared to surrender everything to him—your strength and your weakness, your pride and your shame, your wisdom and your questions—everything must be laid at the gate. Once your hands are empty, walk directly through him, and your journey to manhood will begin."

"Gerasimos, thank you. This is so helpful." Once again

the monk had managed to humble me—an essential exercise for any man who would walk in strength.

"Tell me, David, what is the greatest need in the world today?"

I hesitated. "World peace?" I squeaked, like some nervous beauty queen.

The monk sighed. "We need more great men! Every problem facing our world would vanish if—"

I heard what sounded like another cough, or was it a groan? Then two loud clicks and the phone went dead.

"Gerasimos? Are you there? Can you hear me?" Nothing.

I chuckled to myself. *He probably dropped the phone and doesn't know how to redial.* I hung up in case he figured it out. Then I grabbed my laptop to start blogging about the gate of surrender.

Eight thousand miles away, on a darkened Jerusalem street, two men wearing black-and-white keffiyeh head coverings carried a limp body toward the back of a pickup truck. Moments earlier one of the men had administered a sharp blow to the victim's head, knocking him unconscious. The assailants placed the black-clad body into the bed of the truck, covering it with a heavy wool blanket. The pair jumped into the cab and drove away.

There was only one witness to the attack—a heavyset man with a thick beard and curly locks. He was wearing a topcoat and fedora, even though the evening was mild. His misshapen face gave evidence of a beating at some time in the past. The man was carrying a cane, and with a slight limp he walked to the spot where the assault had taken place. He bent down and retrieved a mobile phone, which had become separated from its battery. The man reassembled the unit, powered it up, and scrolled to the last number dialed. It was a U.S. number, area code 907. *Alaska*.

Isaac Kassif smiled, turned off the phone, slipped it into his pocket, and began planning his next move.

NOTES

Introduction
1. David Murrow, *Why Men Hate Going to Church* (Nashville: Thomas Nelson, 2005).

Chapter 9: Revelation
1. A lot of people think this verse is about heaven and hell. But to this point in the Sermon on the Mount, Jesus has been focusing on earthly concerns: how we're to treat God and our neighbors. If this verse deals with eternity, then it comes out of left field.
2. The verse before (Matthew 7:12) is the most famous passage in all of Scripture, what we know as the golden rule. Read it for yourself: "So in everything, do to others what you would have them do to you, for this sums up the Law and the Prophets." Doesn't this sound like the end of a sermon? You can almost hear the "amen" coming. So the fact that the sermon continues with this dissonant verse tells us to pay attention to it. It's a clue!

Chapter 11: Discovering the Map

1. However, the monastic region of Mount Athos does exist and is home to twenty monasteries. All the stuff about the ferries, minibuses, pilgrims, four-day permits, and no women allowed on the peninsula is true. And, of course, I actually exist.
2. John Gray, *Men Are from Mars, Women Are from Venus* (New York: HarperCollins, 1992).
3. Anthony C. Deane, *How to Understand the Gospels* (London: Hodder and Stoughton, 1936), 110.

Chapter 12: The Way of All Great Men

1. Note: This is also the first significant quote we have from the apostle Paul in Scripture.
2. The Bible mentions Barnabas, John, Judas, Silas, Luke, Mark, Titus, Timothy, Epaphras, Tychicus, Onesimus, and Erastus as companions and/or disciples of Paul.

Chapter 13: The Journey of Submission

1. Andrew Murray, quoted in Cheri Fuller, *The One Year Book of Praying Through the Bible* (Carol Stream, IL: Tyndale, 2003), March 14.
2. Jamie Lash, professor at Dallas Baptist University, as told in his audio series, Victory Seminar, 1988.
3. Albert L. Winseman, "Religion and Gender: A Congregation Divided, Part II," Gallup Tuesday Briefing, Religion and Values Content Channel, December 10, 2002, www.gallup.com.
4. Dan Erickson and Dan Schaeffer, "Modern Man in Contemporary Culture," in *Effective Men's Ministry: The Indispensable Toolkit for Your Church*, ed. Phil Downer (Grand Rapids: Zondervan, 2001), 18.

Chapter 14: The Journey of Strength

1. Richard Rohr and Joseph Martos, *Wild Man's Journey: Reflections on Male Spirituality* (Cincinnati: St. Anthony Messenger Press, 1996), chap. 4.

2. Paul Coughlin, *No More Christian Nice Guy: When Being Nice— Instead of Good—Hurts Men, Women and Children* (Minneapolis: Bethany House, 2005).

3. See Matthew 19:21; 25:14ff.; 1 Corinthians 3:8, 14–15; 15:40ff.

Chapter 15: The Journey of Sacrifice

1. Larry Crabb, *Sixty-Six Love Letters: Discover the Larger Story of the Bible, One Book at a Time* (Nashville: Thomas Nelson, 2009).

Chapter 16: Where Men Get Lost on the Mountain

1. Laurie Goodstein, "Gay Bishop Is Asked to Say Prayer at Inaugural Event," *New York Times*, January 12, 2009.

Chapter 17: The Map: A Thousand and One Uses

1. Kenneth Blanchard and Spencer Johnson, *The One Minute Manager* (New York: William Morrow, 1982).

Chapter 18: Manliness Versus Godliness

1. Brandon O'Brien, "A Jesus for Real Men," *Christianity Today*, April 2008, 51–52.

2. Four titles of popular men's books: *The Barbarian Way* by Erwin McManus, *Unleashing Courageous Faith* by Paul Coughlin, *Risk* by Kenny Luck, and *Wild at Heart* by John Eldredge.

3. Stu Weber, *Tender Warrior* (Sisters, OR: Multnomah, 2003).

Chapter 19: The Three Journeys at Church

1. Mark Galli, "How to Shrink a Church," *Christianity Today* online edition, http://www.christianitytoday.com/ct/2009/aprilweb-only/116-41.0.html?start=1 (accessed April 30, 2009).

2. Find out more about Reveal at www.willowcreek.com/reveal.

3. Lillian Kwon, "Bill Hybels Unveils Willow Creek's Future Vision for Multiplied Impact," *Christian Post Online*, http://christianpost.com/church/Megachurches/2007/05/bill-

hybels-unveils-willow-creek-s-future-vision-for-multiplied-impact-02/index.html (accessed May 2, 2009).

4. S. Michael Craven, "Willow Creek's Confession," *Christian Post Online*; http://christianpost.com/Opinion/Columns/2007/11/willow-creek-s-confession-27/page2.html. Accessed 2 May 2009.

5. John Eldredge, *Wild at Heart* (Nashville: Thomas Nelson, 2001).

6. John Eldredge, "Finding Church," Ransomed Heart blog, http://www.ransomedheartblog.com/john/2009/02/finding-church.html (accessed April 30, 2009).

ABOUT THE AUTHOR

David Murrow is an award-winning television producer and writer based in Alaska (you've probably heard of his most famous client, Sarah Palin). He is the director of Church of Men, an organization that helps congregations reconnect with the world's largest unreached people group. His first book, *Why Men Hate Going to Church*, was an instant Christian bestseller, with more than 100,000 copies in print. His efforts have spawned articles in the *New York Times*, the *Wall Street Journal*, and the *Chicago Tribune*, to name a few. You may have seen him on PBS, the NBC Nightly News, or the Fox News Channel, talking about the Christian gender gap. He lives in the forty-ninth state with his wife, three children, and a dachshund named Pepper.

It's Sunday morning. Where are all the men? Golfing? Playing softball? Watching the tube? Mowing the lawn? Sleeping? One place you won't find them is in church. Less than 40 percent of adults in most churches are men, and almost 25 percent of married churchgoing women attend without their husbands. And why are the men who do go to church so bored? Why won't they let God change their hearts?

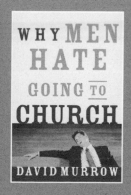

David Murrow's groundbreaking bestseller reveals why men are the world's largest unreached people group. With eye-opening research and a persuasive grasp on the facts, Murrow explains the problem and offers hope and encouragement to women, pastors, and men. *Why Men Hate Going to Church* does not call men back to the church—it calls the church back to men.

Available Wherever Books Are Sold
www.thomasnelson.com

thomasnelson.com